Praise for Monk Dynasty:
An engaging look at monastic history for everyday Christians in the modern world!

Deeply ingrained in the life and mission of the Church, but not always readily understood, is her monastic, religious witness. In Monk Dynasty, John Michael Talbot, with erudition, passion and wit opens a window onto the extraordinary testimony of monastic life in all its many forms. John Michael Talbot comes out of this spiritual current running through the Church and helps all of us wade more comfortably into its life-nurturing waters. This book is a long awaited telling of the story of monks, monasticism and the making of saints.
Donald Cardinal Wuerl, Archbishop of Washington

This is a remarkably rich history of Christian spirituality, focusing especially on the influence that monks have exercised over the practice of ordinary laypeople. Clear and vividly written, it's a page-turner – as engaging as a thriller or a romance – making it unusual and almost unique in this genre.
Mike Aquilina, EWTN Host and Popular Catholic Author

"JMT takes us along on his journey toward understanding monasticism. It is a rollicking ride through history with snacks along the way. Even if we don't join a monastery, we can pick up some of the snacks for our own journey."
Fr. Jerome Kodell, O.S.B. - Former 6th Abbot of Subiaco Abbey

John Michael Talbot is presenting his TV conferences on monastic history and its relevance for today under the surprising title "Monk Dynasty" written in a cheerful language, understandable for all. He develops a vision for a revival of this heritage in our Secular Humanism, showing that renewal has to start within families, so the monk inside every human being can find its special expression in a monastic vocation in a stricter sense. We are grateful for this inspiring book. Monastic History becomes alive and exciting for men and women of our times.

Dr. Notker Wolf OSB, Abbot Primate, San Anselmo Rome

John Michael Talbot provides us an engaging, brief study of monastic history and the evolution of different forms of monastic spirituality. He reflects on the ways that the integration of this rich patrimony finds contemporary expression in the Brothers and Sisters of Charity at the same time as he offers insights into what the witness of monastics of the past and present has to offer for the renewal of Christian life in today's world.

Bishop Anthony B. Taylor, Catholic Diocese of Little Rock, Arkansas

John Michael's view of monastic history "from 30,000 feet" is an exhilarating big picture of how monks have touched our lives. People of all faiths are the beneficiaries of his remarkable distillation of monasticism as a continuum of our faith heritage.

Dan O'Neill, Founder of Mercy Corps, Author of Best-Selling "Signatures: The Story of John Michael Talbot"

Monk Dynasty is right! Monks are ordinary people pursuing an extraordinary call. John Michael Talbot has been living and promoting the monastic lifestyle for decades. Readers who want an accessible tour of monastic history and teaching will appreciate this unique book.

Steve Rabey, Popular Christian Author, Co-author with John Michael Talbot Best-Selleter "The Lessons of St. Francis"

"In an age of declining church membership, it is refreshing to see a Roman Catholic monastic reach out with such joy and authenticity to this new generation. I highly recommend this book to all who would deepen their commitment to Christ, and their journey into the Heart of God."
Abbot Tryphon, All Merciful Saviour Orthodox Monastery – Vashon Island, Washington

In the early centuries of the Church came the great "rush to the desert" as early Christians in both east and west discovered the monastic life and found that the mark of Christian purity was not sterility, but fruitfulness. Now as the postmodern world becomes a desert, we see a renewed interest in that same call to the life of a monk. John Michael Talbot shows that this call is not an escape, but a movement toward the heart of the Crucified and Risen One, for the sake of his Body the Church, and for the salvation of the world.
Mark P. Shea, Author, Mary, Mother of the Son

John Michael weaves important monastic concepts and history into a fun and easy to read text. This is like having John Michael sitting next to you talking through monasticism.
Mark Lanier, Lawyer, Author and Founder of the Lanier Theological Library

Monk Dynasty is no dry history of Christian monasticism. John Michael Talbot brings his usual evangelical zeal to this work, exploring the different phases of the monastic movement as lived through his own experience, with his usual combination erudition and plain talk. This is a fine primer for the new monastics who want to understand the foundations of this noble heritage.
Cyprian Consiglio, OSB Cam., Prior, New Camaldoli Hermitage

Monk Dynasty by John Michael Talbot is a read that is eye-opening, enjoyable and deeply convicting! Musician JMT again becomes serious author John Michael . "The truth is there's a little monk inside every serious Christian!" writes Talbot. If we ARE to be serious about our faith, then how could we possibly IGNORE the nearly 2000 years of monastic tradition as a great source of knowledge and inspiration – and that is exactly what this book offers us. **Tom Booth - Composer, Parish Mission/Retreat Leader, Associate of Music Development for OCP**

MONK DYNASTY

**An engaging look at monastic history
for everyday Christians in the modern world!**

JOHN MICHAEL TALBOT

Published by Troubadour For The Lord Publishing
350 County Road 248
Berryville, AR , USA
72616

All scripture quotes from The New American Bible (Revised Edition) and The English Standard Version (ESV).

Jacket design: Michael Zabrocki
Back Cover photo credit: Peggy Lodewyks, BSCD

ABOUT THE COVER
The icon on the cover was written by Celeste Lauristen as a loving prayer of Little Portion Hermitage including the patron saints of The Brothers and Sisters of Charity.

First Edition
ISBN: 978-1-48356-004-5 (Print)
ISBN: 978-1-48356-005-2 (eBook)
Library of Congress
John Michael Talbot, Berryville, AR

I dedicate this book to my spiritual father, Fr. Martin Wolter, OFM, in deep gratitude for all the loving and balanced teaching he gave me through the years.

May he rest in peace.

ACKNOWLEDGEMENTS

A special thanks to Brandon McGinley, who put my original written thoughts and teachings into a smooth, readable manuscript.

Also thanks to Mike Aquilina and Bishop Anthony Taylor for great editorial assistance.

Special thanks to Mike Zabrocki for the jacket design and his invaluable help in coordinating the details of the publishing of the book for Troubadour For The Lord Publishing.

TABLE OF CONTENTS

Monk Dynasty

CHAPTER 1: INTRODUCTION

Do you need more of "God alone" in your life? Do you need more solitude and silence in the midst of this crazy modern world? Do you need some support from like-minded folks also called to this way of life? If so, you've found the right book!

I like to break the ice at my Catholic Revivals in parishes and dioceses across America by joking that instead of Duck Dynasty, we're going to have a "Monk" Dynasty! And because of my long monastic beard and hair, I also joke that Moses is not with us, that Gandalf has not shown up (for the kids), and that ZZ Top is not in the building (for the rock 'n' rollers)!

Seriously, we have many cultural images of monks and monasteries, most of them rather romantic and ethereal. But few of us, except those who have actually lived in monasteries, understand that they are ordinary places made up of ordinary people with extraordinary calls from God.

It is because of those ordinary, everyday people and places that monastic history itself has so much to teach every follower of Jesus, and every serious seeker of God.

The whimsical title of this little book is "Monk Dynasty." But I hope to bring a serious understanding of monastic history in a way that is informative, fun, and engaging for everyone who reads it. I write as the founder of a new integrated monastic community who has lived this monastic life for nearly 40 years. I have also visited numerous monasteries and communities around the world. I hope that these monastic lessons from the past and the present will help us all to follow Jesus more completely.

Let's start with some basics.

Blood Family

So, what does it mean to be a "Monk Dynasty"? Let's start with that second word: "dynasty." A dynasty is by definition an empire or institution that is passed on through bloodlines. How would that apply to a monastic empire that is made up of men and women who are rarely related by blood?

I have to admit that this stumped me a bit when the concept first came to mind. But then it hit me: All Christians are united by the blood of Jesus Christ! We are part of a spiritual family united by the blood of Jesus that was shed out of the immensity of God's love for each one of us personally, and for us as a united community—a community that has become an empire spread across space and time since the time of Jesus himself.

The concept of a dynasty of blood can be traced to the Old Testament. Psalm 85:5 says of the rule of David, "I will make your dynasty stand forever." Jews understood that this would be fulfilled in the Messiah, and Christians understand that this is fulfilled in Jesus.

Therefore, we often speak of "the blood of Christ" as part of the Eucharist that we celebrate daily, or at least every Sunday, as practicing Catholics. The Gospels tell us: "While they were eating, Jesus took bread, said the blessing, broke it, and giving it to his disciples said, "Take and eat; this is my body." Then he took a cup, gave thanks, and gave it to them, saying, "Drink from it, all of you, for this is my blood of the covenant, which will be shed on behalf of many for the forgiveness of sins." (Mt. 26:26-28)

And St. Paul asks rhetorically, "The cup of blessing that we bless, is it not a participation in the blood of Christ?" (1 Cor. 10:16)

Catholics and Orthodox Christians (that is, all Christians who adhere to the first ecumenical councils of Christian history) believe that in the Eucharist the broken body and shed blood of Jesus is truly present to all who receive. But do we really understand this truth and its implications, or do we just go through the motions at Mass or the Divine Liturgy?

When we celebrate the Eucharist the shed blood of Jesus is being brought from 2000 years ago into the chalice and onto our lips at every Mass! But how can we understand this awesome wonder if we don't first understand the fullness of the Incarnation and the Paschal Mystery?

In the Incarnation God undertakes a divine rescue, through Jesus Christ, for each one of us personally! He comes from eternity into our space and time to reach and rescue each and every creature he uniquely created in His image. On the cross Jesus shed every drop of blood with each one of us in mind. In eternity He knows us each by name. Think of it! As God the Son in eternity He knew every joy and sorrow, laughter and tear, triumph and tragedy in each one of our lives before we ever came into existence. He loves each of us so deeply that he poured out His love by taking on the limitations of our humanity and shed every drop of His blood so that we might be rescued and saved through Jesus Christ. It is an incredibly beautiful story—the most beautiful ever told. And it's all true!

Scripture says: "No one has greater love than this, to lay down one's life for one's friends." (Jn. 15:13)

Why? Because, as the Old Testament says, the life is in the blood. It says of the power of sacrifice to atone: "Since the life of a living body is in its blood, I have made you put it on the altar, so that atonement may thereby be made for your own lives, because it is the blood, as the seat of life, that makes atonement." (Lv. 17:11)

The word "atonement," by the way, literally comes from combining the two English words "at" and "one," or "at-one-ment," and in the religious sense means "being at one with God." Atonement, then is about restoring relationship with the Lord.

Building on this Scripture also says, "According to the law almost everything is purified by blood, and without the shedding of blood there is no forgiveness." (Heb. 9:22)

Now, let's be honest: Few of us in the modern world really understand sacrifice and atonement in the cosmic context of religion. It all sounds a little morbid. When's the last time you sacrificed a sheep, an ox, or goat on an altar for the forgiveness of your sins? See what I mean? We don't really understand the power of sacrifice to atone–to bring us into closer relationship with God.

Of course we have some idea of what it means for somebody to lay down his life to save another. As we mature we begin to understand that despite every person's shortcomings, most parents would give up their life for their spouse and children. I often use the movie *Saving Private Ryan* to illustrate how life-changing it is for someone to lay down their life for another. In the movie the paratrooper Private Ryan was deeply aware that the commander sent to rescue him–Captain Miller–had died in order that he might live the entire rest of his life. As the movie closes, Ryan asks his wife the moving question, "Have I lived a good life?" This was Miller's dying request, that Ryan life a good and worthy life in return for his sacrifice.

We can apply these same recognizable principles to the religious context. Jesus pours out his life blood to rescue us from our slavery to self-absorption and sin that separates us from God and from everyone around us. It is the ultimate example of God's love for us. It is personal. It is intimate. And, when we really reflect on it and understand it, it is radically life-changing. All Jesus asks of us is to live a good life in exchange for His ultimate sacrifice. It is nothing more, but also nothing less, than an exchange of one life for another.

But Jesus is not merely a man. He is God! His death is the exchange of God's Son—His very Self—for each one of us. It is Captain Miller's sacrifice in *Saving Private Ryan* made infinite and eternal. God loves each one of us so much that the infinite and eternal God died so that each of us might live. God is given for each human being personally. This enables us to share now in His divinity through His great gift of love. Through this divine gift we become fully human again! How can we dare to take that for granted?

And unlike Captain Miller, Jesus actually rose from the dead! Death could not be victorious over the God of life! In the resurrection Jesus manifests once and for all the victory of life over death, forgiveness over judgment, justice over vengeance—the victory of all the things every human heart is created to long for.

But you cannot have resurrection until you have death. And the death of Jesus on the cross has a significance that is nothing less than stunning once we really take time to meditate on its saving power.

Scripture says clearly, "In him we have redemption by his blood, the forgiveness of transgressions, in accord with the riches of his grace that he lavished upon us." (Eph. 1:7-8) And: "But now in Christ Jesus you who once were far off have become near by the blood of Christ." (Eph. 2:13)

Apostolic Succession and Succession of the Saints

The sacrifice of Christ's blood is not only personal. It is also communal—a "family affair!" It is passed on from one generation to the next from the time of Christ until today, and forever until the end of the age. That is to say, it is a dynasty. But any good dynasty needs rules of succession. In the Church there is both an apostolic succession, and a succession of the saints that is recognized in the church.

St. Paul says, "(We) are members of the household of God, built upon the foundation of the apostles and prophets, with Christ Jesus himself as the capstone. Through him the whole structure is held together and grows into a temple sacred in the Lord; in him you also are being built together into a dwelling place of God in the Spirit." (Eph. 2:19-22)

Similarly on the theme of building a family structure, St. Peter writes that "(we are) like living stones, let yourselves be built into a spiritual house to be a holy priesthood to offer spiritual sacrifices acceptable to God through Jesus Christ." (1 Pt. 2:5)

We place the stone of our life squarely on the stones—those holy men and women—who have come before us all the way back to the foundation of the apostles and prophets with Jesus as the cornerstone. Lean too far to the left or right, or try to place our stone high up in the air with no support, and we fall to the ground and break to pieces. But we don't just imitate the past. Like Star Trek, we must boldly place the stone of our life "where no stone has gone before!" Each life contributes new experiences to the dynastic tradition.

This means that all of us—clergy and laity, regular Christians in the world and consecrated monastics and religious—are all part of the great spiritual family in Christ. None is better than the other. We are all part of "a chosen race, a royal priesthood, a holy nation, a people of his own, so that you may announce the praises" of him whom called you out of darkness into his wonderful light. (1 Pt. 2:9)

Dynastic succession also applies to leadership. We know that Jesus chose the 12 Apostles from the first larger group of serious disciples, and then appointed Peter as the first among them. Already in Scripture we can see a succession of that apostleship. The record of early Church history says, "They appointed presbyters for them in each church and, with prayer and fasting, commended them to the Lord in whom they had put their faith." (Acts 14:23)

The Fathers of the Church indicate very clearly that this continued as "apostolic succession," from one bishop to the next, so that any bishop to this day can trace his apostolic lineage all the way back to Jesus himself. What could be a surer guarantee that the unadulterated teaching of Jesus would be handed on than face-to-face, from one leader to the next? This can be already be seen as the New Testament was being written, with leaders like Clement of Rome and Ignatius of Antioch and primary documents like the Didache—*The Teachings of the Twelve Apostles*. These early Church leaders had access to the men and women who *knew* Jesus, and to the words they wrote. How much confidence it should give us to be able to trace our spiritual lineage to such people! And it was from the authority of the Church, guided by the Spirit and Apostolic Succession, that the Scriptures were eventually compiled and given to the entire world.

It's no mistake, of course, that the leaders of our "blood dynasty" are often called "mother" or "father." In a real way these people are our spiritual parents, connecting us to our ancestors (and descendants!) in the Faith. So in our Catholic Christian family, our "dynasty," we have lay and clerical moms, dads, and grandparents who can be traced all the way back to Jesus and the Apostles, who worshipped God the Father as the bride of Christ. How fortunate we are!

Monastic Family

If it is true that the Christian spiritual family becomes a dynasty through the blood of Christ, it is also true of monastic families in a more specific and focused way. A monastic family is united in God the Father, Jesus our Brother, and Mother Church as exemplified by Mary, the Mother of God Incarnate in Jesus. But like the Church, we are also united in teachers, fathers, and mothers who hold the place of Christ in the monastic community until He returns. All Christian monastics are brothers and sisters in their unique monastic calling in Christ, and all are connected through the ages by a lineage of spiritual parents and teachers of the Faith.

A monastic family is guided on earth not only by the Spirit who leads us unto all truth but also by a spiritual father or mother—often called an Abbé and Amma in the Christian East, or an Abbot and Abbess in the West. A monastery is not only a building; it is a living community, alive with the breath of the Spirit, and guarded from the gates of hell through communion with St. Peter, to whom Jesus promised the power of the keys. Every spiritual father and mother shares in that promise in proportion to their communion with the successors of Peter and all the Apostles in the power of the Spirit.

This is also true of specific spiritual families and movements within the greater Church. All through history the Church has been renewed and revived by such families and movements of the Holy Spirit. They manifest what popes have often called "an eternal springtime" for the Church, keeping this ancient spiritual family in Christ forever young.

Study Questions

1) Do we really understand the significance of the blood of Christ in the Incarnation of the Word 2000 years ago?

2) Have you ever had someone give their life for you? A parent, or a peacekeeper, or a soldier? What does it mean for you to understand that God has given his life for you personally in Jesus Christ?

3) Do you ever feel unloved by others, or by God? How does it help to truly consider and understand the personal love of God for you and me through the shed blood of Jesus Christ?

4) Do you see yourself as part of a spiritual family united by the blood of Jesus Christ, or is the Church just a religious organization for you?

5) How does the notion of a specific spiritual family within the greater Church have an effect on your life with God and with others in Christ? How does the concept of a specific monastic spiritual family with its own charism of the Spirit impact your life within the Church today?

6) Are we experiencing the eternal springtime of the Holy Spirit in our life and in our communities within the Church? Are we open to genuine revival and renewal in Christ and the power of the Holy Spirit within the Church?

CHAPTER 2: MONASTIC BASICS

My path to Catholic Christianity was twofold. First was the path of the Church fathers through whom the Christian Scriptures were given by God to tell the story of Jesus Christ and the earliest Church. Second was the path of monasticism, which in this day and throughout history has represented a radical charismatic renewal for the Church. These paths led me to the contemporary Catholic charismatic renewal, which has embodied much of the Spirit-filled fire of the historical patristic and monastic movements.

These paths were mysterious, but the voice summoning me was very real. Somehow the Spirit was calling me to a way of life not usually visible to the average American Christian. I didn't choose it. It chose me!

My journey to monasticism started when I visited a public library in Munster, Indiana, to look for books about Christian communities. I felt called to live in community, but I had no idea where to start. First I found the Amish, then the Mennonites and Quakers, but then I stumbled across a book by Thomas Merton called, "The Silent Life." This one text eventually led me to a study of all monastic movements through history. It took me decades to work through libraries of books and to visit countless monasteries of various traditions to understand the mysterious calling that God had placed in my heart. Eventually, I founded the Brothers and Sisters of Charity, a new integrated monastic community for all states of life—married and single, young and elderly, consecrated and lay—within the Catholic Church.

The truth is there's a little monk inside every serious Christian! St. Francis said, "The world is my cloister, my body is my cell, and my soul is the hermit within." Earlier in Church history, St. John Chrysostom said that any serious Christian is a monk, whether married or not! What a wonderful concept! That's why the Catholic, Orthodox, and Eastern Christian Churches have always considered monasticism the mystical and contemplative heart of the catholic, or universal, Church.

This same idea applies to individuals just like it applies to the Church. Monasticism is at the heart of Christian living—not always visible or apparent, but always there nevertheless. We might not live in monasteries, but simply by virtue of being Christians we carry this spiritual core within us. So, it's appropriate for all of us to study a bit of monasticism, even if we've never set foot in a monastery! After all, as St. Francis told us, the world is a cloister for constant communion with God through Christ.

Let's look at some of the basics of monasticism.

Monks

In this book we are discussing the notion of a "Monk Dynasty." We have explored the notion of a Christian spiritual "dynasty" established through the blood of Jesus Christ. But we have yet to look at that first word: "monk." So let's take a few pages to examine what the word "monk" really means.

"Monk" comes from the biblical Greek μόνος (*monos*), which means "alone," "one," or "only." A good example is found in Matthew 14:23: "And after he had dismissed the crowds, he went up on the mountain by himself to pray. When evening came, he was there alone."

It was applied first in monastic history to hermits because they were, after all, alone. Next, it came to be applied to a community of hermits who lived in the wilderness, met together as a larger group once a week for prayer and Eucharist in a common chapel, and shared a common meal in a common house. Later, it applied to those who lived in the wilderness, "alone together," in large monasteries where early monks lived in groups of ten or more in a common house, or in larger dormitories of ten beds per section, and came together daily for common prayer, work, and meals. Eventually, this model—the early version of the form of monasticism that has come to dominate—expanded to those who lived in urban monasteries.

One of the common characteristics of being "alone" in this way has generally been consecrated celibacy, whereby one renounces earthly marriage for the sake of a spiritual marriage to Jesus alone. (This can also be found in non-Christian monasteries where monastics make a temporary or permanent commitment of celibacy.) This is not absolute, however. Some of the early monks of the desert were married, but chose to live in continence (what we might call "as brother and sister") either together or apart. And the monastic pattern often developed to include whole monastic villages made up of sections for monks, female monks, and families. This sometimes occurred organically, as hermits attracted disciples and entire villages grew up around the monastic complex; but in the Celtic pattern monastic evangelists simply converted entire villages to Christ. The wonderful lesson for modern Christians is that monastic life is not limited to a particular type of person or state of life; anybody in any stage or state of life can be called to it!

Hermits

Another important word, from which we get "hermit," is the Biblical Greek ἔρημος (*eremos*), meaning "wilderness, "solitude," or "desert." We can find it throughout Scripture. It is used of John the Baptist in Matthew 3:1-3. "In those days came John the Baptist, preaching in the wilderness of Judea... For this is he who was spoken of by the prophet Isaiah when he said, 'The voice of one crying in the wilderness: Prepare the way of the Lord, make his paths straight.'"

It is also used to describe Jesus' lifestyle pattern of solitary contemplation and evangelistic ministry. Matthew 4:1 says, "Then Jesus was led up by the Spirit into the wilderness to be tempted by the devil." Or Luke 5:15-16 says, "The report about him spread all the more, and great crowds assembled to listen to him and to be cured of their ailments, but he would withdraw to deserted places to pray."

These scriptures reveal to us that even in the life of Jesus Christ there existed a need for times of more intensive solitude and silence, not to mention community with the disciples and apostles, to balance the times of public ministry to the constantly present crowds. Jesus remains the model for all Christian monastics.

Cenobites

When the average Western Christian thinks of monastic life, he or she likely envisions large communities of men or women—Benedictines, Augustinians, Franciscans, and so on—living together to pray, work, and share meals daily, but also to reach out to the outside world with some form of ministry. In the Christian West we often think of fortress-like complexes that house the great monasteries of our history. In the Christian East it is more like a monastic village within walls in the wilderness. This more community-oriented monasticism means folks living "alone together." It is a lifestyle described by the Biblical Greek κοινωνία (koinonia) or κοινόβιον (koinobios), and is often translated "communion," "community," or "common life." It was later Latinized as "cenobite," or "cenobitic," which means "common" and "ordinary life." A good example is the description of the first Christian community in Jerusalem that became the model of common monastic and any later Christian communitarian life. Acts 2:42 says: "They devoted themselves to the teaching of the apostles and to the communal life, to the breaking of the bread and to the prayers."

Consecrated Celibacy

We have also seen that hermits and monks most often embraced consecrated celibacy. Jesus speaks of this call when He says, "Not all can accept [this] word, but only those to whom that is granted. Some are incapable of marriage because they were born so; some, because they were made so by others; some, because they have renounced marriage for the sake of the kingdom of heaven. Whoever can accept this ought to accept it." (Mt. 19:11-12)

Virgins and Widows

The discipline of celibacy has also applied to consecrated virgins and widows. Paul pastorally applied the teaching of Jesus when he said, "To the unmarried and the widows I say that it is well for them to remain single as I do." (1 Cor. 7:8)

The word he uses is the Biblical Greek παρθένος (*parthenos*), or "virgin." This is the root of the word Parthenon—a temple to a virgin goddess. Paul continues:

"If any one thinks that he is not behaving properly toward his betrothed (Greek **παρθένος**, *parthenos*—virgin), if his passions are strong, and it has to be, let him do as he wishes: let them marry— it is no sin. But whoever is firmly established in his heart, being under no necessity but having his desire under control, and has determined this in his heart, to keep her as his betrothed, he will do well. So that he who marries his betrothed does well; and he who refrains from marriage will do better." (1 Cor. 7:36-38)

Another time for celibacy is after the death of a spouse, or in widowhood. Paul says to Timothy, his spiritual son: "Honor widows who are real widows." But he goes on with some fairly realistic restrictions. "If a widow has children or grandchildren, let them first learn their religious duty to their own family and make some return to their parents; for this is acceptable in the sight of God. She who is a real widow, and is left all alone, has set her hope on God and continues in supplications and prayers night and day; Let a widow be enrolled if she is not less than sixty years of age, having been the wife of one husband." (1 Tim. 5:3-9)

With both virgins and widows Paul seemed to be not only a Christian idealist, but also a practical pastor with obvious experience in human nature!

Separated and Divorced

Paul also addresses the all too often modern phenomenon of separation and divorce:

> To the rest I say (not the Lord): if any brother has a wife who is an unbeliever, and she is willing to go on living with him, he should not divorce her; and if any woman has a husband who is an unbeliever, and he is willing to go on living with her, she should not divorce her husband. For the unbelieving husband is made holy through his wife, and the unbelieving wife is made holy

through the brother. Otherwise your children would be unclean, whereas in fact they are holy. (1 Cor. 7:12-14)

But he allows for separation if the unbelieving partner wishes it.

If the unbeliever separates, however, let him separate. The brother or sister is not bound in such cases; God has called you to peace. For how do you know, wife, whether you will save your husband; or how do you know, husband, whether you will save your wife? (1 Cor. 7:15-16)

All that is to say that many who are separated or divorced today choose to live in celibacy. It is a new, but also ancient, path to monastic life. This can be either temporary or permanent. But it is never an excuse for separation or divorce from one's spouse. In today's culture of unraveling families, Christians need to strengthen, not weaken the family.

Moving Forward

Today most Christians are not called to celibacy. But all are called to chastity! The word "chastity" refers to sexual abstinence outside of marriage and fidelity within marriage. Celibacy, then, is just one way of living out chastity, and marriage, to which most Christians are called these days, is another. In today's libertine secular humanist culture chastity can seem harder and harder to live out, and more and more countercultural. But that's exactly why it's so important for us to be a prophetic witness by joyfully living out this teaching!

Lastly, monasticism is not a uniquely Christian phenomenon, but it was one that was easily baptized by Christianity. Some of this is seen in the Egyptian Therapeutes, a Jewish monastic movement, from which we get the word "therapy." Some actually conjecture that they were influenced by the Theravada Buddhist monks who came to Egypt after Alexander the Great opened trade routes between the Far East and the Mediterranean. Without getting lost in the weeds, we can point out that monastic expressions can be seen in Hinduism, Buddhism, Taoism, and the Essenes, a Jewish sect around the Dead Sea. After Christian monks went to the Far East the crosspollination continued as Hindu monks established outreach ministries, and even Islam embraced monastic ideas in the Sufi movement.

Our focus in this book, however, is Christian monasticism. In the subsequent chapters we will treat the saints and the movements who embodied, invigorated, and expanded Christian monasticism.

Study Questions

1) The word "monk" means "one" and "alone." Are we living for God and God alone? Or is our focus on Jesus scattered and diluted through a focus on this passing world?

2) The notion of a hermit who lives in solitude is not applicable for most of us today, but we all have needs for solitude and silence. Are we taking regular times for being alone with God in solitude? This could be in an annual retreat, a monthly day of recollection, or 20 to 30 minutes every day.

3) Even hermits lived in colonies. Are we finding strength and support from other like-minded people within the Church who also feel called by God to a greater experience of solitude and silence?

4)   Eventually, monks gathered into intentional communities where they prayed, worked, and shared meals together every day. For most of us we find this within our own nuclear family, which is the domestic church. Is our family a daily source of spiritual strength for us? Are we taking appropriate steps to foster healthy spiritual disciplines for prayer, study, and meals every day, week, and month?

5)   Some of us are called to celibacy, either as virgins from an early time in our life or as widows after the death of a spouse. Many are called to celibacy after the break-up of a relationship. Some couples are called to celibacy. Do we see consecrated celibacy as a living vocational alternative?

6)   Do we see marital, or conjugal chastity as prophetic in our life? How do we nurture and protect it so we might better proclaim this prophetic message with the fidelity of our life as well as with our words?

CHAPTER 3: THE EGYPTIAN DESERT

There are many lifestyle vocations in the Church. There are also many ways to live the monastic life. I think we will find inspiration from the ancient monks for every vocation in Christ and the Church today. Far from being archaic examples from the past, they are timeless voices for the present as we continually build up the Church until the coming of Christ! I discovered this personally through study and visiting many different types of monasteries and communities.

In my study of Christian monasticism I quickly decided to visit some monasteries. I needed to see the ideas put into practice. My plan was simple: head south from my home in Munster, Indiana, toward Indianapolis, and visit monasteries I had read about. The first was a Franciscan retreat center called Alverna, where a priest lived whom I had met years ago at an Evangelical conference led by Francis Schaeffer. Then I planned to go to the beautiful Saint Meinrad Archabbey in southern Indiana. From there I wanted to go to Our Lady of Gethsemani in Kentucky, where Thomas Merton had lived as a monk. I ended up not only visiting these places, but taking up residence and then building a hermitage on the grounds of the Alverna Retreat Center with the Franciscans in Indianapolis.

It was from a combination of study and lifestyle that I was introduced pretty quickly to the writings of the Desert Fathers. I first read *The Sayings of the Desert Fathers*, and from there proceeded to other compilations of their teachings and biographies. It took me a couple of years to get to the Middle East to actually see the various traditions of Eastern monasticism lived on the ground in the

Holy Land. What I discovered was amazing, and life changing! And it changed me for the better! I hope it will inspire you too!

The Desert

Christian monasticism began, like Christianity itself, in the Middle East. Specifically, it emerged as a call to the solitude and silence of the desert. Because our study of monasticism is from the Christian perspective there's no better place to begin than with Jesus!

As He foretells times of trial and tribulation in the secular world Jesus teaches, "Then those in Judea must flee to the mountains." (Mt. 24:16)

But it is not only during times of trouble that Jesus tells and shows us to go into solitude and silence. Jesus Himself went into the desert for intense times of prayer to prepare for his public ministry.

Scripture says, "Then Jesus was led up by the Spirit into the wilderness to be tempted by the devil." (Mt. 24:16) And in Luke: "The report about him spread all the more, and great crowds assembled to listen to him and to be cured of their ailments, but he would withdraw to deserted places to pray." (Lk. 5:15-16)

So there is an intimate link between solitude and silence, on the one hand, and active proclamation of the Gospel among the crowds who are hungry for God on the other. Those who try to minister without first being ministered to by God have nothing to give. You cannot give what you don't have. You cannot fill another's canteen for the journey if you have not first been to the divine well of the Spirit to fill your own.

As we saw in the last chapter, the word for "desert" in biblical Greek is "*eremos*." But it doesn't always mean the desert in a literal way.

It simply means a wilderness, or a deserted place, and is often translated that way in various editions of the Bible. So throughout Christian history monastics have gone into solitude and silence in a way consistent with the environment and the geography of the region in which they live. Sometimes that is an actual desert, as is the case in the Middle East. But in Europe, or parts of Russia, China, India, or Africa the wilderness might be mountainous, or the deep woods. What's important is not a literal translation of the word "desert," but the notion of being in solitude and silence in a way that is undistracted by the noise and chaos of the secular world.

Still, it cannot be denied that the first expressions of Christian monasticism were found in the deserts of Egypt, Palestine, and Syria. There is no great mystery to this. The greatest solitude in the Middle East is found in the desert.

It must also be admitted that there is a mysterious allure to the desert as compared to other wildernesses around the world. In the desert there are few visual distractions, and the silence is almost overwhelming. Not so in the forest, where there is often ample wildlife, foliage, and water. In the desert one is forced to live at the bare minimum of the essentials needed for survival. It strips one back to the very basics of physical life so that the spirit might be free to soar to the heavens unencumbered. Lastly, the examples of many of the prophets of the Old Testament, John the Baptist, Jesus, and even Paul give a clear biblical precedent for withdrawing into the desert. The allure of the desert remains primary for Christian monastics who, when given the choice, will often choose the desert over other wildernesses for foundation sites.

Egypt

Perhaps surprisingly, it is in the deserts of Egypt rather than Palestine that Christian monasticism first rises to prominence. It is this Egyptian, or Coptic, monasticism that becomes the paradigm on which all other monastic expressions are based. Why?

First, there are the examples of the great founding fathers of monasticism such as Saint Antony the Great and the hermits who discovered and preceded him, such as St. Paul of the Desert. From these the whole tradition of the Desert Fathers and Mothers grew up and inspired Christian monasticism all around the world.

But there is another reason, less obvious to non-Coptic Christians: the example of the Holy Family withdrawing into Egypt during Herod's persecution after the birth of Jesus Christ. Egyptian, or Coptic Christianity takes great pride in the historical and traditional tales of the Holy Family in Egypt. The presence of Mary, Joseph, and the Christ Child are essential to understanding Coptic Christianity, and permeate the great Christian monastic movement that was raised up by the Spirit there.

Types of Coptic Monasticism

There is no one way to live the Christian life, nor is monasticism homogenous in its expression. It is unity in diversity that gives the Church its strength. Ancient monasticism amplifies this with an intense spirituality that still speaks to all of us today. We all need times of silence and solitude to balance the constant noise of modern living. We all need to find a way of living in greater Christian community in order to provide the support we really need to stay faithful and alive in our life with Christ. We all need to find stability as we move from one place to another far more frequently than we did in previous generations.

Monasticism in Egypt developed organically. It is found in three major forms, and a fourth that is legendary, but not unreal. They are:

1)   Solitaries (what we in the West would call hermits and recluses) exemplified by St. Antony and St. Paul of the Desert.

2)   Colonies of hermits called Sketes, originally from *Scetis* or *Shiheet* (meaning "to weight the heart"), *Kellia* (meaning "the Cells") founded by Ammoun, or Lavras or Lauras (Greek: Λαύρα; Cyrillic: Ла́вра) meaning literally the alleys or souks in a typical Eastern town, exemplified by St. Macarius.

3)   Cenobites based on the Koinonia of St. Pachomius.

4)   Hermits in total solitude in the desert who are never or rarely seen by other monks, and who live almost miraculously without human means by the hand of God and through the assistance of His angels. Some think they are only legendary, or imaginary. Others testify to their real existence in the desert even today. There are collections of their lives in book form.

The three major patterns are also found in geographically distinct places in Egypt. It's a bit confusing for the average Westerner! In Egypt, "Upper Egypt," is actually south at the beginning of the Nile River which flows down (north) into "Lower Egypt," where it empties into the Mediterranean Sea. In the West we usually referred to, "upper," as north, and, "lower," as south. In Egypt it is exactly the opposite!

Lower Egypt

We find the first monks in Lower Egypt in monastic colonies of hermits in the Wadi El Natrun valley: Sketes for more interaction and Kellia (or, the Cells) for greater solitude. This valley was the home of most of the Desert Fathers and Mothers whose sayings and lives come down to us today. They eventually lived in isolated hermit cells by themselves, or with a young monk or two in formation throughout the week. They prayed the ninth hour, or 3 PM, outside their cells so they could hear, but not necessarily see one another praying. This was the first expression of monastic common prayer. They came together on Saturday for a Synaxis, or "gathering" prayer and Agape Meal, and a Eucharist on Sunday. Then they gathered weekly provisions before walking back to their hermit cell for the rest of the week.

Modern Applications

I find this a fascinating example for Christians in the modern world today. Few of us can live in an intentional community where we pray, work, and share a meal together every day. Even so, this hermit colony pattern of life provides a great example for us. Think of it: These ancient monastic patterns provide powerful models of how modern families or friends can share daily life together, then go to their local parish church weekly for a small group or ministry for spiritual nourishment in addition to Sunday Mass. So, the hermit colonies of Egypt are not as archaic or unapproachable as we might think!

St. Antony

The Life of St. Antony was written by St. Athanasius of Alexandria, and is considered the first popular biography of a saint in Christian history. These are called "hagiographies," and are filled with what seem to be fantastical tales and larger than life legends in addition to the facts of the saint's life, in contrast to our more factual modern notion of biographies. Even so, we shouldn't discount even the most fanciful stories; many saints' lives were filled with miracles that sound outlandish to modern ears!

The Life of Antony was the first of its kind, and became the pattern used by all others thereafter. It became an ancient version of a "runaway best seller!" St. Athanasius knew him personally, and had real devotion to the holy man. It is considered even by modern secular historians to be quite accurate. Here are some of the known facts:

St. Antony was born the son of wealthy Christian parents in the Lower Egyptian village of Coma in 251. Upon their deaths he inherited a small fortune in land and belongings. At this time he heard and was convicted by Jesus' exhortation to the rich young man in Matthew 19:21: "If you would be perfect, go, sell what you possess and give to the poor, and you will have treasure in heaven; and come, follow me."

That's exactly what Antony did! He eventually set his sister up with a group of female ascetics and sought solitude for himself. Antony went first, though, to live with a nameless elder ascetic to learn the way of discipleship before retiring into strict solitude. This shows St. Antony's humility and obedience, and it illustrates that there were others pioneering the monastic way of life before him. So, while St. Antony is called "The Father of Monks," and became without question the most popular example for future monastics, he was not the first.

St. Antony was one of the first Christian ascetics to strike out far into the desert to find the solitude he craved. Naturally his uniqueness attracted unwanted attention—both from Christians seeking spiritual guidance and from the Devil, who has always hated the devotion to Jesus demonstrated by people like St. Antony. It's said that the Devil would tempt Antony with apparitions of silver and gold and beautiful women, but without fail the saint would see through these ruses. Once, Antony was beaten within an inch of his life by little demons in a cave, but he was revived by the people of a nearby town.

While St. Antony's desert adventures might seem extreme, one of the most important lessons we can take from his life is balance. Even as he pursued solitude he went out to Alexandria to help Christians facing persecution there—and to seek (unsuccessfully) his own martyrdom. And even as he fled the crowds that sought him, he soon began permitting communities of desert monks to form around him—some of the first Christian monastic communities!

I could go on forever with stories from the life of St. Antony. Here are just a few legends and lessons.

Lessons from St. Antony

From the life of Saint Antony we see some great lessons that apply both to monastics and to any Christian seeking to live an authentically spiritual life.

1) One of the most striking themes in St. Athanasius's *Life of St. Antony* is the treatment of spiritual warfare. Perhaps for the first time in Christian writing we see a detailed treatment of spiritual combat with demons and devils. St. Antony was besought both physically and psychologically by demons throughout his life. Yet his mind remained sharp and clear, and his body remarkably remained supple and healthy even into old age.

Beyond the standard teachings of defeating the Devil through humility and trusting in the victory of Jesus by His shed blood and empty tomb, Antony gives us something unique. One takeaway from these descriptions is that demons can neither tell the future nor bi-locate. Sometimes, they appear to do so by foretelling the arrival of guest to the hermit's cell. But St. Antony emphasizes that they are neither omnipresent, nor omniscient: They're just really smart, and very fast! Demons are not to be taken lightly, but the humor of this point reminds us they are only creatures, albeit spiritual ones, under the ultimate power of God and definitively defeated by the love of God shone in the shed blood of Jesus Christ.

2) Another valuable lesson from the life of St. Antony is how to beat spiritual boredom. Like all of us, he sometimes struggled to maintain his prayer without his mind wandering. The Lord revealed to him an image of a monk who would pray for a while, then work for a while before returning to prayer. An angel said to him, "Go and do likewise, and you will be saved." The text simply says that he went and did likewise, and was saved! This is typical of the pithy, and often whimsical style of the teachings of the Desert Fathers.

3) Antony describes the balance among prayer, work, and recreation by analogy to the tension of the bowstring. The bow must be strong with tension in order to shoot an arrow straight and far. But the tension must be let off the bow from time to time, or the bow will snap and break. Likewise, there needs to be the creative tension in prayer and work, but the tension must be relieved from time to time through rest, relaxation, and recreation. This little illustration demonstrates the practical wisdom of the otherwise heavenly spiritual warrior. Do we find such balance in our life?

4) The story of Antony going to Alexandria to minister to persecuted Christians who were imprisoned is very significant! Even the great hermit Antony broke his solitude and silence when the need for gospel charity demanded that he encourage his brothers and sisters in the great city. In the same way, we are called to sacrifice our own desire for spiritual comfort when our brothers and sisters need assistance and encouragement in Christ.

5) One last legend is worth mentioning: Antony's discovery of an earlier and greater hermit living in the solitude of the Egyptian

desert—St. Paul the Hermit (c. 228 - c. 343). Interestingly, only St. Jerome mentions this legend, and some even doubt its veracity. Even so there are real lessons we can learn from it.

In the story St. Antony is humbled when an angel brings to his mind that there exists an even greater hermit than himself in the Egyptian desert. Antony begins to search through the wilderness to find if it is true, and discovers St. Paul the Hermit living in a remote cave, dressed in a monk's habit of woven palm leaves, and living on daily bread supplied by the ever-present ravens of the region. Paul had been there for nearly 100 years! For a day and a night they shared fraternal fellowship that can only be described as heaven on earth. Antony departs, and comes back to find that St. Paul has died, and that lions are helping to dig his grave peacefully with their paws. Antony is deeply touched by this fellowship with the great Hermit, and although he has accomplished so much in his life (Antony truly is the "Father of Monks") he demonstrates great love and humility toward the simple and pure Paul.

Ammoun

A lesser known figure of Lower Egyptian monasticism is Ammoun. There are two great Desert Fathers by the same name; we will discuss the first, Ammoun of Nitria.

What distinguishes Ammoun is that he is one of the only married Desert Fathers! He was married for 18 years before he, with the consent of his wife, withdrew to a celibate monastic life. As far as we know there was no divorce or annulment; this became an acceptable pattern for married couples who heard the call from Christ to freely and with mutual consent enter monastic life.

Ammoun's emotional separation from his wife, though, was not total. The *Paradise of the Fathers* says, "Twice in the year he used to go and see his spouse; and he died in his virginity, and his wife likewise brought the years of her life to an end in purity." This also implies that they were "continent," or never engaged in sexual activity.

Nevertheless, monastic separations can be problematic. In his treatment of virginity and celibacy St. Paul says that while both celibacy and marriage are good, celibacy is better because it frees a person from family responsibilities to pursue ministry for Christ. But he also allows for mutually discerned periods of abstinence in marriage when he says, "Do not deprive each other, except perhaps by mutual consent for a time, to be free for prayer, but then return to one another, so that Satan may not tempt you through your lack of self-control. This I say by way of concession, however, not as a command." (1 Cor. 7:5-6)

Historically the Church has allowed for so-called "continent marriages," and for one or both members of married couples to withdraw into monastic or consecrated celibacy with free mutual consent. But the Church is more cautious of this nowadays. The theology of marriage has developed to require consummation for validity, and we take more seriously the possibility of after-the-fact feelings and accusations of abandonment

But otherwise Ammoun was known for being one of the most rigorous hermits in Egypt. And he is considered the founder of Kellia, or The Cells on remote land he discovered with—you guessed it!—Antony, where monks seeking even greater solitude withdrew.

Arsenius

Arsenius is also one of the more recognized Desert Fathers, known for extreme poverty, ragged monastic clothing, long hours of prayer, a frugal diet, and tears that flowed so copiously that they wore trenches in his skin! Perhaps even more striking is that prior to withdrawing into the solitude of the desert he was a Roman senator! Before becoming a monk he was accustomed to opulent wealth and luxury.

There is a story in the *Paradise of the Fathers* where a monk criticizes Arsenius for not living quite as poorly as the others when he was sick:

> They used to say that [on one occasion] when Abbâ Arsenius the Great fell ill in Scete, a priest went and brought him to the church, and he spread a palm-leaf mat for him, and [placed] a small pillow under his head; and one of the old men came to visit him and saw that he was lying upon a mat and that he had a pillow under his head, and he was offended and said, "And this is Arsenius lying upon such things!" Then the priest took the old man aside privately, and said unto him, "What labour didst thou do in thy village?" and the old man said unto him, "I was a shepherd." And the priest said unto him, "What manner of life didst thou lead in the world?" and he said unto him, "A life of toil, and sore want." And when the old man had described all the tribulation which he had endured in the world, the priest said unto him, "And here what manner of life dost thou lead?" And the old man said unto him, "In my cell I have everything comfortable, and I have more than I want"; and the priest said unto him, "Consider [the position of] Abbâ Arsenius when he was in the world! He was the father of kings, and a thousand slaves, girt about with gold-embroidered vests, and with chains and ornaments round their necks, and clothed in silk, stood before him; and he had the most costly couches and cushions [to lie upon]. But thou wast a shepherd, and

the comforts which thou didst never enjoy in the world thou hast here; but this man Arsenius hath not here the comforts which he enjoyed in the world, and now thou art at thine ease whilst he is troubled." Then the mind of the old man was opened, and he expressed contrition and said, "Father, forgive me; I have sinned. Verily this is the way of truth. He hath come to a state of humility, whilst I have attained to ease." And the old man having profited went his way.

It seems that for every story of extreme self-sacrifice, you can find another of human mercy with the Desert Fathers. They simply refuse any strict or legalistic categorization! This also brings out that Christian asceticism is never an end unto itself. It is always practiced properly when in the context of deepening our personal love relationship with Jesus Christ in full communion with the Church, and others in a monastic family. For everyday folks today, that might easily translate to their nuclear family, parish, or work environment.

St. Pachomius

St. Pachomius (292–348) is the Father of communal monastic life, or Cenobitism. Some have pointed out that while Antony's eremitism (individual asceticism and solitude) and semi-eremitism was developed in a time of persecution, St. Pachomius's Koinonia, or community life, was developed *after* the Diocletian persecution, when Christians living together was a safer option.

After being raised in a pagan family and going through a conversion to Christ in 313 after having been conscripted into the Roman military, he began living as a hermit under an elder spiritual father named Apa (Abbot) Palamon, a disciple of St. Antony. After finding the abandoned village of Tabennisi, he heard God's voice telling him to build a monastery there because He was going to bring him many brothers. He shared this with Apa Palamon, who went to help him in establishing the new monastery. After the aged elder died, an angel appeared to Pachomius pointing to a monastic rule and an infant's hood garment, indicating that God was calling him to make the stricter hermit life available to a broader group of people.

After some initial hesitations, Pachomius organized his community along military lines into houses of ten monks according to their skills—carpentry, iron working, farming, baking, and so on. Each house was led by an elder called a dean. The monks met in their house for prayers, and also gathered in the central monastery church for Mass, daily evening prayer, and a common meal. Then they met on Sundays to hear Pachomius's biblical teachings. The entire community was under the leadership of a central Abbot, or Apa, who was also responsible for the spiritual leadership of daughter monasteries founded by the central motherhouse.

This movement was numerically larger than that of St. Antony, but collapsed after a struggle over leadership succession when Pachomius didn't appoint his primary disciple, Theodore, as his successor due to some disobedience. But in recent years there has been a resurgence of appreciation of St. Pachomius as the Father of Koinonia, or cenobitic monasticism.

There is a story about St. Pachomius that should interest founders of communities today. In the early days St. Pachomius loved his brothers so much that he did all of the work to support the community. After a while it became apparent that the other handful of monks were not going to pitch in and do their fair share. St. Pachomius had a suspicion that he was being taken advantage of, but did not want to be uncharitable, so he went to the local bishop and laid out the case before him. The bishop confirmed that the other brothers should be given an ultimatum either to do their fair share of the work, or to go away. St. Pachomius relayed the bishop's words to the brothers, who rejected the advice. So St. Pachomius, with the authority of the bishop behind him, ejected the slothful brothers from the community.

After this unfortunate episode, God blessed him with an abundance of vocations for the new community. St. Athanasius, the Patriarch of Alexandria, visited both Antony and Pachomius, and praised them both. Pachomius was more of a teacher than the typical Desert Fathers, and instructed the brothers on a wide range of monastic subjects using a remarkable knowledge of Scripture. Pachomius's communities grew to be the largest monastic phenomenon in Egypt—so successful that when Pachomius and Antony met the hermit confessed that, had he began his vocation after Pachomius, he would gladly have joined Pachomius. That is quite a compliment from the Father who was hands-down considered the greatest monastic in Egypt!

The lessons here are significant.

1)   Pachomius first submits to a spiritual father or elder (Apa Palamon) before becoming one himself. Do we submit our spiritual life to direction through obedience to a spiritual father, mother, or elder?

2)   He also comes down from his personal height of eremitism in order to minister to many more through a communal, or cenobitical, community. Do we sacrifice our own desires in order to minister to others?

3)   He doesn't do this through his own will, but in obedience to God, Who directs him through an angel with the confirmation of his spiritual father. Are we willing to turn our back on our individual will and accept direction from spiritual leaders, and God?

4) He does not build from nothing, but rebuilds a derelict village at Tabennisi. Are we willing to Christianize the ruins of the secular world?

5) Pachomius's first attempt proceeded by fits and starts, but he kept going through the encouragement of his bishop. How do we face failure in community and ministry?

6) He uses his basic military skills to organize a community in a manner familiar to him. Do we use organizational skills in our faith community or ministry?

7) Pachomius uses an ingenious pattern of small groups amid the larger monastery in his monastic dynasty. Do we cultivate meaningful relationships in manageable groups in our larger social and spiritual communities?

Desert Teachings of St. Antony

The teachings from the various sources of the Desert Fathers and Mothers are many; it would take a lifetime to read, pray, live, and absorb them all. And even then we would only scratch the surface. I will list here just a few from St. Antony, as the quintessential Father of Monks.

Work and Prayer

"'Lord, I want to be saved but these thoughts do not leave me alone, what shall I do in my affliction? How can I be saved?' A short while afterwards, when he got up to go out, Antony saw a man like himself sitting at his work, getting up from his work to pray, and sitting down and plaiting rope, then getting up again to pray. He heard the angel saying to him, "do this and you will be saved." At these words, Anthony was filled with joy and courage. He did this, and he was saved.

"Whoever you may be with, always have God before your eyes. Whatever you do, do it according to the testimony of the Holy Scriptures. In whatever place you live, do not easily leave it. Keep these three precepts and you will be saved."

The Cell

"Just as fish die if they stay too long out of water, so the monks who loiter outside their cells or pass their time with men of the world lose the intensity of inner peace. So like fish going towards the sea, we must hurry to reach our cell, for fear that if we delay outside we will lose our interior watchfulness."

Solitude and Community

"Put an arrow in your bow and shoot it. Shoot another. Shoot yet again. If you bend the bow so much it will break it. It is the same way with the work of God. If we stretch the brethren beyond measure they will soon break. Sometimes it is necessary to come down to meet their needs."

Poverty

"Those who renounce the world but want to keep something for themselves are torn in this way by the demons who make war on them."

The World and Madness

"The time is coming when men will go mad, and when they see someone who is not mad, they will attack him saying, 'You are mad, you are not like us.'"

Revelation of Thoughts

"If he is able to, a monk ought to tell his elders confidently how many steps he takes and how many drops of water he drinks in his cell, in case he is in error about it."

Modern Egyptian Monastic Revival

One of the wonders of modern Christianity in the Middle East is the revival of Egyptian Monasticism. From a Sunday School Movement instituted by the late Pope Shenouda III of Alexandria of the Coptic Church great interest in monastic life was generated among highly skilled and professional men. The ancient Sketes, St. Antony's and St. Paul's monasteries outside of modern day Cairo, and even the monasteries of Upper Egypt began to experience revival and growth that was a phenomenon of the Holy Spirit.

Today the number of monks in the main monasteries has risen to hundreds where not long ago there were only tens, or even handfuls of surviving monks. The monks now oversee thousands of lay employees in their farms and bakeries, which support the monastic movement. They minister to thousands of pilgrims daily. And apparitions, signs, and miracles of healing and conversion are common.

Of course, since the rise of extremist Islam such activities have been negatively affected, and some even fear for the safety of the monks. Let's pray that this phenomenon of the Spirit in modern monastic revival will continue and will bring the Christian faith many saints–but hopefully not many martyrs. We pray for peace, and that this revival might spread to Coptic monasteries wherever they are found!

Study Questions

1)   Where are the "deserts" in our personal environment?

2)   Are we willing to take radical steps in establishing a solitary and silent environment for deep prayer?

3)   Do we understand spiritual warfare?

4)   Do we have balance, moderation, and discernment in our spirituality?

5)   Do we seek real community with like-minded Christians in a way that is appropriate to our state of life?

6)   Are we willing to submit to the guidance of a spiritual father or mother as a real elder in our spiritual life?

7)   Are we open to modern revival in our midst? Are ready to give our lives as martyrs if need be?

CHAPTER 4: PALESTINE

Do you ever wish you could just once "walk where Jesus walked" to revitalize your Christian faith? Sometimes our modern Christianity, especially in America, seems cut off from its historic roots and from Jesus himself. Of course, we use Jesus' name and Scripture to validate our modern, Western Christian experience. But sometimes we feel at the same time that we are creating something so novel and new that it is no longer authentically Christian at all. I felt the same thing, and visited the Holy Land early in my conversion to Catholic (and monastic) Christianity. It has grounded me throughout my life in a way mere books can never do!

My primary encounter with desert monasticism is through my pilgrimages to the Holy Land. In Palestine I was first able to visit St. George's Monastery in the Wadi Kelt valley between Jerusalem and Jericho. A wadi is essentially a dry river valley in the deserts of the Middle East. There I was ushered as a special guest with other religious through the cliff-hanging monastery churches, dwellings, and hermitages before walking down the valley riddled with caves where thousands of hermit monks once lived. It was simply mesmerizing—a scene from a fantasy movie come to life. I was hooked! I also visited later religious houses and monasteries, but the allure of the ancients of the deserts of Judean Palestine called me ever deeper. At one point I stayed in hermit caves once occupied by a saintly Franciscan friar—an honor that permanently impacted my then-young life.

History

It was inevitable that the charismatic success of the outpouring of the Holy Spirit on the monks in Egypt would eventually spread throughout Christendom. And it spread like wildfire! It started when the monks of Egypt migrated to the land of Jesus in Palestine.

Gaza

The first place where Egyptian monasticism transplanted into Palestine was in Gaza. Today we hear of infamous "Gaza Strip" and its role in the ongoing tensions between Palestinians and Israelis. Today it is one of the most densely populated stretches of ground on planet earth! But this was not always the case. Biblically, it is the place along the Mediterranean near Sinai where the Philistines originally dwelt before being displaced by the migration of the Jewish people. Of course most of us remember the famous battle between the young shepherd boy, David, who slew the Philistine giant warrior Goliath with a mere slingshot.

Hilarion

The first monastic to migrate from Egypt to Gaza was Hilarion (291-371). Interestingly, the word "Hilarion" means "joyful" and is where we get the modern word "hilarious!" So, Hilarion was a joyful monastic!

Hilarion, like so many others, was a disciple of Antony the Great in Egypt. He migrated to a very dangerous place in Palestine, bringing with him a monk's habit bestowed on him by St. Antony himself. He built a hut of reeds, and lived on a diet so meager that he had to add some oil to it to preserve his eyesight. Yet it was in the midst of this self-sacrifice for Christ that he developed a reputation for joyfulness!

After he had lived in the wilderness for 22 years, he became famous in Syria Palaestina (Palestine), the Roman province where the Holy Land was located, attracting a multitude of pilgrims. A veritable monastic city was built around him as lay people settled and a group of disciples formed. Even though the push of the crowds drove Hilarion to more remote locations, the crowds followed. After returning home to Antony's hermitage in Egypt he went to Sicily, and then to Dalmatia in Southeast Europe, and finally to Cyprus where he died in 371.

Hilarion's life followed a pattern: He would withdraw to solitude, attract crowds, build a monastery, and work many miracles in the name of Jesus. Then he would be overwhelmed by the crowds and the fame that crushed in on him, robbing him of the solitude and silence in which he found the empowerment of the Spirit in the first place. He would withdraw again to get away from the reputation of being a miracle worker, and the pattern would start all over again! This pattern repeated itself from Gaza to Egypt to Sicily and eventually to Cyprus.

One interesting wrinkle in the story is that after he left Palestine, the governor of the province sent troops to retrieve him. The Roman authorities wanted him due to the religious tourism he generated wherever he settled. He had become an accidental holy outlaw from the secular Roman government! It turned out Roman Palestine eventually regained his body from Sicily after he died. So, the "law" finally caught up with Hilarion!

Hilarion teaches us that we should be humble, but can't outrun the destiny God has for us. He also teaches us to be joyful through it all! Lastly, he shows us that monastic stability and peace is far more than an external reality. Hilarion was stable and peaceful in his life with Christ, despite his frequent travels.

Barsanuphius and John

Gaza produced even more monastic saints. We also read about Barsanuphius (died 540) and John (died two weeks after Barsanuphius), both of whom also migrated from Egypt. Their gift was condensing the sayings of Desert Fathers in letters to and from Barsanuphius, John and other monastics seeking the wisdom of the desert from two great elders who had actually lived it. A veritable treasure house of spiritual wisdom resulted.

Reading their letters is educational, inspiring, and more than a little amusing! They are both mystical and pastorally practical at the same time. On the surface, they contain an incredible working knowledge of the teachings of the Desert Fathers and Mothers. But more than that, time after time we can see the letters bring the inquiring monks to die to their old selves and rise up a new creation in Christ. It's almost as if you can hear them thinking, "Don't you get it yet?" This is not unlike Jesus' rebuke of the apostles in the Gospels. It is so simple in concept, but far from easy in practice. It takes a lifetime to even begin to get it.

And this is the greatest gift of all monastic life. How can we find the extraordinary in the ordinary things of life in Christ with others? The letters repeatedly teach that monasteries are filled with monastics who are really just ordinary folks responding to an extraordinary call from Christ. Over and over we read them saying in essence, "I've told you this before. Now just do it!" But they never lose patience, and they persevere in their ministry of teaching.

Even today monasticism remains what St. Benedict would later call "a school of the Lord's service," where those who really desire to die to their old selves through the cross of Christ and rise up a truly new creation in Him are provided a communal environment in which to do so in a very intentional way. It is a more specific way of living out our baptismal promises through obedience to a spiritual father or mother in community.

Dorotheus of Gaza

Another great Palestinian monastic saint is Dorotheus of Gaza (c. 505 – c. 565). His name comes from the Greek Dōrótheos meaning "God's Gift", from δῶρον (dōron), "gift" and θεός (theós), "god." And what a gift from God he was!

The surviving written work of Dorotheus of Gaza includes classic monastic teaching, and is considered among the few primers for Eastern Christian novice monks to this day. We Western monastics would also do well to study his teaching, and more and more are doing so.

One of his truly unique teachings is incredibly relevant to our modern "blame game" culture. We tend to make excuses for our own shortcomings while holding everyone else to an impossibly high standard of moral perfection. This permeates our polarized politics and religion. It is dangerous and deadly. Dorotheus taught radically on taking self-responsibility for conflict, calling it "self-blame." Since this carries so many negative psychological connotations, I prefer to simply call it "taking responsibility."

Dorotheus teaches this by presenting a hypothetical scenario in a typical Eastern Christian monastery. I will paraphrase the teaching in my own words.

Suppose you're walking through the monastery minding your own business and you come across another brother who becomes very angry, screaming and yelling at you for something you didn't do. What will our reaction be? According to our fallen nature, we would probably defend ourselves, and perhaps even react aggressively in kind. As natural as that might be, Dorotheus says that you can never live in peace in any monastic or Christian community if that's the way you respond.

Of course, maybe the brother is having a bad day and we just happened to come along at the wrong time and bear the brunt of his frustration and anger. But Dorotheus takes it further. He teaches that we should ask ourselves what we might've done to provoke such a response. Perhaps we did something that we are not aware of? Perhaps we did something to the brother years ago, and it has never been sufficiently healed to the forgiveness and repentance called for by Jesus Christ? Perhaps it's just our countenance or the way we carry ourselves that aggravates this particular brother? Or maybe even we did something to someone else a long time ago, and this is God's way of getting our attention to bring healing in other areas of our life?

Only after we take responsibility for "cleaning our side of the street," as they say in Alcoholics Anonymous, will we be able to dialogue in a way that is truly healing. Jesus teaches that we are to seek a brother out one on one if we feel that they have done something against us, or if we suspect that we have offended them.

That's why Dorotheus doesn't stop at taking self-responsibility. He goes on to say that if we really love our brothers and sisters, we must take the risk of humbly correcting them through healthy dialogue when they do something that is wrong in the monastery. This chapter is aptly called "Correction." We could call both the chapters on "self-accusation" and "correction" as powerful paradigm shifts for what we moderns call "conflict resolution."

This is tricky business! It's hard to find the balance where self-defense leaves off and self-sacrifice picks up.

Essentially, what this means is learning how to dialogue in a selfless and self-emptying way in Christ, not for the sake of justifying ourselves but of truly communicating in Christ with others. First we listen, and really listen from the heart. Then we talk. Talking before we really listen and empathize is simply "talking at," rather than "communicating with" another human being just like us. What we've discovered in our monastic experience is quietly, calmly, and gently correcting another brother or sister when they are clearly doing something improper is very effective not just in resolving the issue, but in being Christ to that person. We are also careful to let those who have leadership responsibility take the primary role. The job of the rank-and-file is to support.

In one-on-one dialogue we also learn how to share rather than argue, respond rather than react, dialogue rather than debate. This might mean bringing our problem to another by saying something like: "When you act this way for that, this is how it makes me feel," rather than simply accusing them of being wrong. We also readily admit that we might have misunderstood the communication or action, or we might be wrong and need to ask forgiveness from them.

This is radical! It's incredibly counter-cultural, not to mention counter to our natural tendencies.

Judea

St. Sabbas, St. Euthymius, and St. Theodosius

Monasticism in Palestine moved naturally from Gaza on the Mediterranean coast to Judea in the inland desert along the Jordan River and the Dead Sea. The two archetypical saints are St. Sabbas (439-532) and St. Theodosius the Cenobiarch (c. 423-529)

St. Sabbas became the Archimandrite (a superior abbot supervising other monastic abbots) of those living the semi-eremitical life, and St. Theododius, though beginning as a hermit, was the Archimandrite of those living the Koinonia, or cenobitical monastic life. St. Sabbas was first the humble disciple of the elder St. Euthymius (377-473), who directed him to St. Theoctistus (died 467) (not to be confused with St. Theodosius). Only later did he become his coworker, and the one who passed on his teaching to others.

The spread of the monastic life throughout Judea was phenomenal. While the monastery of Mar Saba still exists outside of Bethlehem in Judea today, there are over 120 monastic ruins throughout the region, not counting northern Israel, that can still be explored by the serious monastic or archeological student today. There were monasteries literally around every hill and tucked inside every wadi. This seems incredible to us today! But the archeology is clear.

The Lives of St. Euthymius and St. Sabbas come to us through Cyril of Scythopolis. These Lives are filled with typical stories about their asceticism, miracles, and monastic patterns of life. But they also describe these saints' struggles as monastic leaders in the Christianized Roman Empire and in the Church as they faced schisms, heresies, and even violent struggles.

Within the Church they faced two heresies: Origenism and Monophysitism (or Miaphysitism). Euthymius lived through two key Ecumenical Councils—Ephesus in 431, and Chalcedon in 451—and was remarkable in his humble obedience to the Church and in his intuition of orthodoxy. Sabbas was his humble disciple, and embodied much of the same.

In attempting to explain orthodox Christianity to the Greek philosophical world, Origen had almost inadvertently accepted certain ideas foreign to traditional apostolic Christian teaching. Origenists accepted not only the notion of an immortal soul, but also the pre-existence of the soul, and the ultimate salvation *even of the souls in Hell* through Christ. In the legitimate development of Christian doctrine we accepted the immortality of the soul, but rejected the other two as being incompatible with apostolic Christianity.

Monophysitism (Greek: μονοφυσιτισμός from μόνος (*monos*), "only, single" and φύσις (*physis*), "nature" and/or "person") rejected the Ecumenical Council of Chalcedon in 451 AD which confirmed the truth of Jesus Christ's One Person and two natures—human and divine. Ironically, they considered themselves staunch defenders of St. Cyril of Alexandria's position of One Hypostasis, or divine and human Person in Jesus, against the heretic Nestorius, who taught two *"prosopons"* (masks), or persons in Christ. In the process the Monophysites confused the one *hypostasis* with the one *physis* (another Greek word employed for 'person,' from which we get the English, "physical," or "nature") of Jesus.

If this sounds confusing, that's because it is! Such theological issues were actually less confusing to those accustomed to the Greek language of the time. And praise God that the divisions this created are now being healed by a dialogue of mutual respect and love by everyone who embraces both the full divinity and humanity of Jesus Christ. The details of ancient disputes are not unimportant, but they are not as important for theologians using today's languages and developments to bring the Gospel of Jesus Christ in a unified way to a modern world that needs Him so badly.

For us modern folks living in pluralistic societies we often wonder what difference it makes, saying "Live and let live" or "To each his own." But to more homogenous societies of the past such controversies tore at the unity of the community and consequently of the Church. There is wisdom in greater unity, of course, but there is also a danger of lapsing into judgmental legalism. Good Church and monastic leadership finds the balance between truth and love, doctrinal purity and leniency, penance and forgiveness, unity and diversity.

Regarding Monophysitism, the various Greek words used for "person" mean slightly different things, and complicate the delicate but essential theological understanding of the Incarnation. While both heresies considered themselves orthodox, and the differences began with good will, they hardened into intractable positions fortified by pride, anger, and even violence. That is where the problem really comes to fruition.

St. Sabbas, St. Euthymius, and St. Theodosius found themselves embroiled in both Origenism and, to a lesser degree, Monophysitism. In particular St. Sabbas eventually faced a group of Origenist monks who broke away and started their own "New Lavra" not far from his original Great Lavra. Even violence erupted at times. While this all sounds academic, or even silly from the safe distance of the future, it was gut-wrenchingly painful in the days of the early Church and monastic life. Today we tend to be more understanding in trying to mend broken fences. But back then it was terrible, with people actually breaking apart the communion of the Church we share in Christ.

I bring up St. Sabbas, St. Euthymius, and St. Theodosius not only to explain the greatness of the monastic impact on Church life in Palestine, but to illustrate two points: first, how important orthodoxy is to good monasticism, and second, how to keep going despite divisions in the Church or even in monasteries. We face the same issues in different ways today. These great monastic saints of ancient Palestine had not only great meekness, but also great strength to keep the Faith in Christ united and pure. They help show us the way, truth, and life of Jesus Christ.

Study Questions

1) How do we deal with the tension between solitude and silence on the one hand, and the need to minister on the other?

2) How do we approach recognition, or even fame?

3) Do we faithfully pass on the teaching of elders, or do we consider them outdated and irrelevant?

4) Do we take full responsibility for failed relationships, or do we try to blame others?

5) How do we deal with conflict resolution in our family, church, or community? Are we able to correct one another out of love? Are we defensive when corrected?

6) How do we understand the need for orthodoxy?

7) How well do we cope with division in community?

CHAPTER 5: URBAN MONASTICISM

Modern life is urban life! We can dream about the monasticism of the desert wilderness, but the fact is that most of us live deeply embedded within the urban or suburban life of the modern age. For the vast majority of us monastic spirituality and its connected lifestyle only make sense if they can be translated into the "urban jungle" of modern living. But have no fear! Monastic history provides a model for those of us who live the hectic pace of the city.

Monasticism was destined to spread from the desert 'countryside' to the city. Folks left the growing corruption of urban centers, and then returned to their hometowns to spread the purity of the Gospel of Jesus with the authority of a life radically changed in Christ. They could not hoard such a remarkable gift by keeping it entirely to themselves; it had to be shared!

Jesus says, "I do not ask that you take them out of the world but that you keep them from the evil one. They do not belong to the world any more than I belong to the world." (Jn. 17:15-16)

So, there is a distinction between being in the world, and being "worldly." St. John explains, "For all that is in the world, sensual lust, enticement for the eyes, and a pretentious life, is not from the Father but is from the world. Yet the world and its enticement are passing away." (1 Jn. 2:16-17)

Pope Francis extols the symbol of the redeemed city in his encyclical letter *Evangelii Gaudium* (The Joy of the Gospel) when he states, "It is curious that God's revelation tells us that the fullness of humanity and of history is realized in a city. We need to look at our cities with a contemplative gaze, a gaze of faith which sees God dwelling in their homes, in their streets and squares." And even one of the modern classic works on desert monasticism by Derwas J. Chitty is called *The Desert a City*, remarking that when tens of thousands of monks settled in the deserts of Egypt and Palestine they became a new holy city.

To use the common saying, we are "in the world, but not of the world." Monasticism grappled with this tension as well. Two saints exemplify it very well: St. Basil and St. Augustine.

St. Basil the Great (329 or 330–379)

St. Basil is called "The Father of Eastern Monasticism." And his "Asketikon" (Ascetical Discourses), or what are often called "Rules," are to Eastern Monasticism what The Rule of St. Benedict is to the Christian West—a foundational text. Even St. Benedict acquiesces to their preeminence, referring to them by name at the end of his great Rule as being greater guides than his own "little rule for beginners." (RB 73:5)

Basil, like many of the great saints we discuss in this book, was born into a wealthy family, but later liquidated the family fortune and distributed it to the poor. This is not unlike the news of a modern celebrity doing a 180-degree conversion from a life of opulence and sin today to a life of religion and God. He was raised in and stayed in central Asia Minor—modern Turkey.

Owing to his family's wealth, Basil was well-educated and well-traveled for his era. He studied in Constantinople and Athens and developed a reputation for intelligence, which he turned into a respectable career in rhetoric and the law. While his parents were devout Christians, Basil was lukewarm in his faith. Under the influence of his local bishop and his saintly sister, Macrina, a fire for the Lord was kindled within Basil. He traveled more, this time to Egypt and Syria and Palestine and Mesopotamia to learn the ways of the monks of those lands.

Along with Macrina, Basil established a monastery on his family's estate at Annesi. While he likely would have been perfectly happy to stay in his community reading and writing the days away, Basil ended up being summoned to Church administration, a calling that ultimately led to his consecration as Bishop of Caesarea.

St. Basil was a notable innovator in the area of social support for the poor and vulnerable. Not only did he liquidate what remained of his family's fortune while he was bishop, he also built the Basiliad, a kind of massive hub for social services, including housing, work training, financial support, and healthcare. When he wasn't tending to the poor, he was zealously defending orthodoxy against the Arian heresy.

Lessons from St. Basil

The lessons we can learn from St. Basil of Caesarea are many, and mighty!

First, after his baptism he uses the secular education he received for the cause of Christ. This teaches us that nothing in our life is ever wasted. Everything we bring to the cross must die, but it is resurrected in a new form in and through Jesus Christ! St. Basil's secular training was a powerful tool as a theologian, monastic founder, and Patriarch of the Church.

We must also use our natural gifts and talents as tools for spreading the Gospel of Jesus Christ. But, we must fully let them go— that is, let go of our egoistic attachments to them—so that Jesus can use them in entirely new and surprising ways! We sometimes make two mistakes. The first is to so completely disavow our natural gifts, talents, and education that we rob ourselves and others of these tools. The second and less obvious mistake is to only incompletely bring our natural gifts, talents, and education to the cross of Christ! Consequently, we try to follow Jesus, but still in our own way. Inadvertently, we try to remake Christ according to our image, rather than allowing Jesus to remake us according to His.

Basil had to leave the secular life in order to fully discover his religious life in Christ. He left his native home and made a pilgrimage to visit the great monastic hermits who had lived the ascetical life for many years. After living completely by himself as a hermit in Pontus, he placed himself under Eustathius, a famous hermit, who was already considered the Father of Cappadocian Monasticism. But Basil differed with him both on doctrine and on ascetical extremism. Basil then returned home to found a more moderate and balanced evangelical form of life based more squarely on the life of Christ and the teachings of the New Testament.

What about us? Are we willing to leave all that is familiar to us to answer the call of Christ? Are we willing to leave family, friends, and our native home in order to discover a new spiritual family, friends, and our heavenly home while sojourning on the face of this earth? We must be willing to make radical breaks with past patterns in order for new patterns, according to the pure Gospel of Jesus Christ, to be firmly established for the rest of our life, and into eternity!

But this does not mean that past relationships are void. Rather, they are fulfilled and multiplied! Another powerful symbol of St. Basil is family relationships. St. Basil's first monastery was his own family! This was a common pattern in early Christian monasticism. Entire families would embrace Christ according to the monastic pattern of life, and turn their family estates into monasteries. This is what happened with St. Basil at Annesi. In Basil's case the monastery included his mother Emmelia, his brother Peter, and his sister Macrina. Peter was the superior of the monastic family, and his sister was considered the holiest of them all. And so she was Peter's successor after he died at an early age. Basil's fame came later after he became a bishop, where he used monastic training and patterns of life throughout his diocese.

The question arises: How are our family relationships in Christ? Have our families really accepted the radical call of Jesus Christ? Are we able to see our brothers and sisters as holier than ourselves—our leaders and superiors in Christ? Do we see our families as obstacles to holiness, or instruments used by Christ to make us more holy? Do we allow our family to be brought down to worldly standards, or do we use the gifts of the Church and the saints to raise our family to higher standards? And even more radically, do our Christian homes become little monasteries in the Church and the secular world?

The greatest lesson in Basilian Monasticism is from the Basiliad, or what the ancients wonderfully called The New City. The Basiliad was an immense monastic city, and was considered an astonishing wonder of the world in its day. It was a great center for monastic training, education, medical care, and social assistance for the needy, as well as a place for daily prayer, preaching, and sacramental celebration. Every monastic, community-based cenobites and individual eremites alike, took turns in evangelical gospel ministry to those most in need of God's love, truth, and mercy.

The Rules and The Asketikon

The so-called Longer and Shorter Rules of St. Basil are not really formal monastic rules at all, at least not in the Western sense. Yet they provide one of the earliest basic rules for all monastic expressions in the Christian East. More precisely, they are ascetical discourses based on questions and answers about ascetical monastic or evangelical life. The first chapters are more general for all Christians, and the subsequent chapters apply specifically to those living in community. While clearly addressing monastic life, St. Basil really uses the Evangelical Life of Jesus and the first Christians as his example.

The rules are too lengthy to give a full commentary here, but they are most interesting in that they provide one of the earliest specific applications of gospel and monastic teaching to actual communities. There is nothing particularly striking about the teachings themselves, except that they are specific, detailed, and well-organized. It is a foundational document in monastic history, both East and West.

Perhaps the most remarkable aspect of Basil's monasticism is his apparent rejection of the hermit life. He says, "For how will he practice the virtue of humility, if there is no one to whom he may show himself humble? How will he show pity, if he is cut off from the society of others? Or how will he show forbearance, if there is no one to oppose his wishes? But if someone says that instruction in the Holy Scriptures is sufficient for right conduct, he is like one who learns how to weave, but never weaves anything, or is taught the smith's art, but never deigns to put into practice what he has learnt." (The Long Rules Q. 7)

But it would be an oversimplification to say that Basil forbade the eremitical life. In fact, both Basil in the East and Benedict in the West began as hermits, as did Pachomius who founded community life before either of them, and they concluded by living and teaching the cenobitical life in monastic Koinonia. Benedict reached a different conclusion about hermits that has proven to be the paradigm in both the East and the West: Cenobitical life is the more common monastic life that should be a school which prepares at least a few for the semi-eremitical life, or even the strictly eremitical reclusive life. The hermit life is considered by Benedict to be the highest monastic call.

Basil, while not being so permissive, still found space for hermits. For him the cenobitical life is not only more common and desirable for the many, but is the superior way of life. But even Basil is said to have included hermits and semi-hermits around the Basiliad, provided that they also came in to do at least some ministry with other monks in the monastic hospital, school, or social care center. A lesson we can take from this is the importance of making space for others' experiences, even when don't precisely fit our ideas. Solitude cannot be an escape from our responsibility in love to minister the Gospel of Jesus to others.

Study Questions

1) Do we find the balance between contemplative prayer and apostolic action in our life?

2) Do we spend appropriate periods of time in sacred silence to empower our apostolic ministry?

3) Do we try to do ministry without the power of prayer behind it? You cannot give what you do not have! You cannot evangelize until you have been evangelized. Conversely, prayer must have an outlet in some form of ministry to keep it from becoming self-absorbed. If the dammed up water is not allowed to flow, eventually the dam will burst and great harm will be done downstream.

For the average Christian monastic, and for most Christians in general, we need the empowerment of prayer to fully invigorate our ministry, but we also need the outlet of ministry to keep our prayer from stagnating.

St Augustine of Hippo

St. Augustine is known mainly for his influence on Christianity due to his remarkable collection of writings. But Augustine was also part of the development of monasticism as it spread into the city, making him a huge contributor to the entire future of consecrated life in the Western Church. He shows us how to bring a truly serious Christianity to our family, church, and culture to revive them in Christ. He also is a great example of how we can face the unraveling of our own culture with the solid faith, hope, and love that only Jesus and the Catholic Church can bring.

After his legendary conversion and baptism by St. Ambrose in Milan, Augustine adopted a monastic life at his family estate at Thagaste in modern day Algeria. He was joined by his mother and the illegitimate son he had with his concubine before his conversion—this family monastic arrangement was actually a common practice in his time for Church fathers who adopted an ascetical way of life.

After beginning his family monastic life at Thagaste he was elevated to the bishopric in nearby Hippo. It is here that the more common Augustinian form of urban monasticism developed and prospered. He wrote a rule for the laity, then invited other clergy to join him; his sister went on to adopt the rule of life for a group of women. But in order to fully grasp its significance we must place it in context.

In Augustine's day the Church in North Africa was in disarray. In contrast to the success in Carthage under St. Cyprian and in Alexandria under St. Athanasius, Algeria and Libya were torn apart by heresies.

The Manicheans taught the dualist heresy that Spirit was good and flesh was evil. The Donatists were schismatic rigorists who taught that those who abandoned the faith under the Diocletian persecution could not be received back, and even validly ordained Donatist clergy did not bring valid sacraments. And the Arians taught that Jesus was fully human but was not fully divine; while he might have enjoyed preexistence, was still a created being, therefore not as divine as God the Father. These false teachings all threatened the full communion of the Church, or the orthodox Catholic teaching that Jesus was the full Incarnation of the Divine Word, and was fully human *and* divine in a world that was created and redeemed by God through Christ.

To combat these schisms and heresies Augustine needed not just theology and the ability to debate, but the example of a radically converted way of life in Christ. Augustine knew that actions speak louder than words. And it was here that his vision for an urban monastic life came fully into play.

Augustine required all of his clergy to embrace a celibate monastic way of life, and to live together in monasteries in the midst of the city where they sought to preach the Gospel of Jesus Christ. They would live the apostolic common life of Acts 2 and 4, pray, celebrate the sacraments, and study the Scriptures before preaching Jesus to others. Bishops were sent from these initial monastic establishments to the various dioceses in North Africa, where the pattern was replicated. And this urban monastic experiment was a success! It slowly spread and reformed the entire region through a return to orthodox Catholic Christianity.

But this Golden Age was short-lived. Soon, the barbarian Goths and Vandals ventured from across the sea to the shores of North Africa. Augustine witnessed cathedrals and churches he had established pillaged and destroyed, bishops and clergy he had ordained

beaten and slaughtered, virgins and nuns he had helped to con-
secrate raped and killed, and the cities he had reached for Christ
plundered and razed. It must have been shocking, frightening,
and demoralizing to North Africans. Some scholars believe that
Augustine himself died from starvation as a result of a prolonged
siege of the city of Hippo. Sadly, Augustine died just three weeks
before his beloved Hippo fell to the barbarians. Some say God
spared him from having to live through such a devastating loss
while still alive on earth.

But the wonder of St. Augustine is his unflinching and remarkable
faith, even in the face of persecution and death. It is this side of
Augustine that we so often and easily overlook. We are tempted
to look only to his great theological writings to understand him,
forgetting his wonderfully brief yet all-inclusive monastic rule. But
in order to fully appreciate this man of faith, we must also understand his struggle to establish the Golden Age of Christianity in
North Africa, followed by its complete unraveling and devastation.
It is there that we really find the strength of the faith behind this
remarkable man.

This speaks volumes to us in modern Western civilization. We live
in a time when we have shifted from a Judeo-Christian moral foundation to a completely secular humanist foundation. America has
been subtly and slowly remade in the course of the last few generations. We have witnessed this most remarkably within our lifetime. Our culture is unraveling, and so are many of the once-filled
churches in our midst. It can be terribly demoralizing to witness
and experience.

But we have a choice. We can bemoan this state of affairs, grumble,
and accuse others, or we can choose to live a positive, faith-filled
life even in the midst of a completely secular humanist society. We
can curse the darkness, or we can light a candle in Christ. Saint

Augustine shows us a remarkable way to do this in our lifetime. I for one choose to follow his example of faithfulness in Christ even as Christianity and civilization seem to be unraveling before our eyes.

The Rule of St. Augustine

The monastic writing that was compiled as the Rule of St. Augustine is remarkable in both its brevity and its status as the earliest written rule for the Western Church. It was first composed as a letter to sisters living the consecrated life, and was later adapted as a monastic rule for men.

The rule was used for the male and female communities founded by St. Augustine. Its influence is clearly visible in subsequent rules of Fulgentius of Ruspe (462/8-527/33), Isadore of Seville (560-636), Caesarius of Arles (470-542), and the Rule of the Master that preceded the later Rule of Benedict. After being absorbed in the West it was resurrected in the 10th and 11th century reforms as a basic monastic rule that provided a workable alternative to the Rule of Benedict for countless communities that stretch all the way to our present day. Not only formal Augustinians of various ways of life, but many other communities under various names, such as the well-known Dominicans, use the Rule of Augustine as their primary religious rule of life.

The rule is utterly remarkable in its brevity and comprehensive scope! In this we see the rule's genius, and what made it so attractive for future reform communities in the Western church.

The great theme of the rule is the common life of love and charity in Christ as defined and lived by the first Christian community of Jerusalem in Acts 4:32-35. But there are a few unique characteristics to the rule which humanize it and make it extremely livable. This is important when considering it against the backdrop of the extreme, virtually superhuman lifestyles of the monastic legends of the East who predate it.

There are a few points which have always stayed with me through my years as a monastic in a new, integrated expression of monasticism.

The first is that, while retaining an emphasis on common monastic life that rules out personal possessions, the rule does not impose a strict uniformity on all its members. It maintains unity in diversity without compromising the most important points of monastic life. It recognizes the frailty as well as the strengths of the members who came from various backgrounds before they entered monastic life.

For instance, in Chapter 1 the rule recognizes, like the Desert Fathers before, that while some might appear to be less poor, they have actually given up a great deal in coming to monastic life from a higher station, while others might appear to live more easily in gospel poverty, but have actually given up less because they came from a lower station in life. That is, with great wisdom it accounts for human frailty. It also guards against the pride of those who, coming from a lower station in life, now get to hang out with those coming from a higher station.

Chapter 2 treats community prayer and the use of the Psalter as something already established in and known to his community, so the actual content of the Divine Office is not mentioned. What is very perceptive is his statement, "When you pray to God in Psalms and songs, the words spoken by your lips should also be alive in your hearts." This teaching will be echoed in later rules in both St. Benedict and St. Francis. It helps avoid vainly rattling off our prayers like a machine gun!

Chapter 3 takes into account the legitimate care of the body. This is almost unheard of in previous monastic writings and rules! While establishing fasting, abstinence from certain foods, and frugal meals taken while listening in silence to spiritual reading and instruction, it takes individual human frailty into account. It again addresses the situation of those coming from wealth or poverty (both spiritual and physical) before they enter monastic life, and the understanding and accommodation given to them because of their background.

In chapters 4 and 6 St. Augustine uses the gospel admonitions found in Matthew 7 for "Mutual Responsibility in Good and Evil" for avoidance of sin, and "Love and Conflict" regarding conflict resolution in the case of sin. Dealing with the temptations to and ramifications of sin had proven to be a huge problem in community, and Augustine builds squarely on the teaching of Jesus as his solution. He recommends mutual encouragement to avoid sin, and personal dialogue when we actually commit sin. That personal dialogue is to be the first charitable step before proceeding to community leaders for more formal discipline.

Chapter 5 of the rule includes a remarkable paragraph about going to public baths! This is in contrast to the previous monastic tradition that exalted the notion that many saints never bathed in order to overcome the tendencies of the flesh. Augustine takes his own culture into account, where public baths are considered normal for good health. But he also puts guidelines in place that they never go to the baths alone in order to avoid the temptation to or the appearance of impropriety.

Chapter 7 addresses "Love in Authority and Obedience," or the leadership of the community. While never using the title "abbot," the rule admonishes the members to view the primary leader as a spiritual father or mother. It also teaches to obey lovingly, not only due to the personal holiness of the leader, but due to the honor of their office, and the Christian belief that God will speak to us personally through leaders regardless of their personalities or personal spiritual successes or failures. But it also admonishes leaders to be loving and kind, as well as strong. Leaders regard themselves as the least of all while members regard them as superior. Gospel charity is found in that balance.

Study Questions

1) Augustine was the master of simplicity and balance. Are we able to adapt the teaching of Jesus, the Church, and the great monastic saints in a way that is simple and livable in our own time?

2) How well do we live the common life of Acts 2 and 4 in our own faith communities and families?

3) Augustine reformed and consolidated the fragmented church of his region through teaching that was first lived in his monastic communities. Does our way of life speak as loudly as our words and theology in the face of heresy, division, and schism within the Church today?

4) Augustine remained faithful in the face of the unraveling of the world around him and the destruction of all he had built in monastic communities and his churches. How do we face the unraveling of our own Western civilization, and the church within it?

CHAPTER 6: SPREAD TO THE WEST FROM EGYPT

St. Jerome and St. John Cassian: Scripture and Spiritual Life

Do you ever wonder why Catholics are sometimes viewed by other Christians and the wider culture as ignorant or disinterested about the Bible? True enough, we often can't even find it on our bookshelves! And we often only passively listen to it at Mass. Yet it's our book! Scripture came forth from the Church, and to read it outside of that context—as if it were any other secular document—is to do violence to its very authority. We hear a huge portion of Scripture in our Sunday and daily Masses, and the early monks prayed all 150 Psalms daily, or at least weekly. Of the Church Fathers, St. Jerome teaches us most compellingly about a truly biblical monasticism.

Do you ever wonder at the wild array of thoughts and temptations that come to your mind and heart? Does your life ever feel disorganized and chaotic? Well, St. John Cassian shows us a way to discover the origin and interconnection of thoughts through an orderly monastic discipline that helps discover the mind of Christ and the simple living of Jesus and the saints.

I remember on my first long pilgrimage to the Holy Land being overwhelmed when standing in St. Jerome's monastic cell in Bethlehem where he translated much of Vulgate Bible, and standing in the complex where the original monastery of John Cassian stood. Somehow that tradition was coming right up from the soles of my feet and through my eyes, penetrating deeply into my heart. But I didn't yet know much about these great monastic saints.

As I began reading through volumes in monastic libraries and accumulating volumes for the community I was founding, I discovered both Jerome and John Cassian. Frankly, I found Jerome caustic and off-putting at first. But after spending some extended quiet time in the very cell in Bethlehem where Jerome translated the Vulgate Bible, I felt a deep connection to him. The spirit of the man touched me. I had to learn more!

For me, John Cassian was simply the name attached to his works the *Institutes* and the *Conferences*. Only slowly did he begin to really make sense—primarily through my own life in an integrated monastic community. Slowly the wisdom of the *Institutes* became clear as we discovered a need for a good monastic rule of life to help us through the often stormy and uncharted waters of forming a new community. Specifically, Cassian's Eight Thoughts started to click into place as I discovered their logic and mystery in my own interior life, and in my communal life with others. What once seemed to be an artificial and untouchable teaching from the past became eminently practical as I sought to live the ancient lives of the Egyptian monks in my own community.

As monastic life spread from Egypt into Palestine and Syria it also spread westward into Europe. It had already moved west into North Africa with Augustine, but it still needed to move across the Mediterranean into southern France, Italy, and the Celtic regions of the Spanish coasts, then into England, Ireland, and Scotland.

Let's focus on two great monastic saints who represent two great tools: Scripture and prayer.

St. Jerome

Jerome is one of the more controversial of the monastic saints. He was not only dedicated and brilliant, but also downright irascible. At the very least he was fiery! Unsurprisingly he managed to create a lot of enemies. While some of these were inevitable due to the uncompromising nature of the Gospel itself, his tendency towards polemics and his hot temper probably created many more enemies he could've otherwise avoided.

Scripture

Jerome is probably best known for the famous quote: "Ignorance of Scripture is ignorance of Christ." And it was Jerome who was the first Christian to translate the Old Testament into the street language of the day, or the Vulgate, from the original Hebrew. Up until that time the Old Testament in common usage was the Septuagint, or the Greek translation. Indeed, it was from the Greek version of the Jewish scriptures that we find the quotes used throughout the New Testament. Scripture, Jerome knew and taught, is essential to understanding Jesus Christ in an authentic way.

But the early Church fathers teach that Scripture must be interpreted in its own context if it is to be properly understood and applied today. That context is the apostolic authority and tradition from which it emerged and through which was compiled. Scripture came forth from the apostles chosen by Christ (Peter, James, John, and so on) and their immediate successors (Paul and their disciples). It was compiled by their successors to whom the Spirit had been promised. To understand Scripture we must also understand the Church through which it was given. To deny the one is to destroy the authority of the other. This is itself clearly scriptural.

St. Paul speaks first of a living apostolic tradition before he even speaks of the inspiration of Scripture when he says to his spiritual son Timothy, "But you, remain faithful to what you have learned and believed, because you know from whom you learned it, and that from infancy you have known [the] sacred scriptures, which are capable of giving you wisdom for salvation through faith in Christ Jesus. All scripture is inspired by God and is useful for teaching, for refutation, for correction, and for training in righteousness, so that one who belongs to God may be competent, equipped for every good work." (1 Tim. 3: 14-17)

Scripture is the earliest written record of the authentic apostolic tradition that was established from the call of Christ and His promise of the Spirit. It is the "canon" or "measuring stick" we use to judge all further development in the Church. Not every specific circumstance we face is found explicitly in Scripture, but the universal principles are there. Nothing trumps Scripture.

There is within that tradition, however, valid development of doctrine. The development of the doctrines of the Trinity or the Incarnation if the Word in Jesus Christ, for instance, are clearly found in Scripture, but the theological development is from the first five centuries of the Church. As specific questions or challenges are met, more specific answers are developed.

There is a difference between development of doctrine and novel additions to doctrine (or its degeneration). A huge oak tree was once a mere acorn. The two look very dissimilar at first glance, but the essential qualities of the oak tree are there throughout its developmental cycle. An oak tree cannot become a pine tree, or even more radically, a dog or horse. The same is true with development of doctrine: It can unfold into a fuller understanding of the Truth, but not into something else entirely—and certainly not into falsehood. This is implied from the beginning, but is first expressed fully by St. Vincent of Lerins, a monastic island off the southern coast of France.

So we see two currents of divine inspiration within the stream of divine revelation: Apostolic Tradition and Scripture. Vatican II reaffirms this long established pattern of the early Church. The third addition is the Magisterium, or teaching authority, of the Church that creates the proverbial third leg of the stool of doctrine. This is seen in the teaching of the early Church from St. Vincent of Lerins, as well as in later greats such as John Henry Newman.

The biblical Greek word used for Scripture is γραφή (graphē). And the word for inspired by God is θεόπνευστος (theopneustos). This comes from two words in conjunction together, θεός (theos), or "God" and πνέω (pneo), or "breath"–similar to πνεῦμα (pneuma), or "spirit." So "inspired by God" literally means, "God breathed." Just like God breathed life into Man before he became a living soul (Gen. 1:7), so must we see the Scriptures through the power of the Spirit, who leads us to all truth. (Jn. 16:13)

The authentic monastic heritage uses Scripture as its primary rule in the context of a community and its leaders truly living in the power of the Holy Spirit–itself within the greater context and leadership of the Catholic Church. Centuries later St. Bonaventure, the great Franciscan Seraphic Doctor of the Church, would affirm that we cannot really study or even begin to understand Scripture without first praying for the enlightenment of the Holy Spirit.

The Life

What makes Jerome interesting is first, his genuine radicalism and unfortunate irascibility in living the ascetical monastic life and, second, his love of Scripture and his calling to translate a version in the Vulgar Latin from the original Hebrew and Greek.

Let's look briefly at the broad strokes of his most interesting life.

Born around 347 in Dalmatia (modern Croatia), Jerome became interested in the Church while studying in Rome as a teenager. He pursued some theological studies, but didn't totally commit himself to those studies until a vision he experienced during a severe illness while traveling through Asia Minor. He went into the wilderness, staying and studying for a while in Chalcis, known for its hermits. This is where the monastic lifestyle stuck like glue to St. Jerome, and he committed to it in one form or another for the rest of his life!

He travelled and studied some more, ending up in Rome as an advisor to and acolyte of Pope Damasus I. It was here that he began work on what would ultimately become his most celebrated achievement—the Vulgate Bible. In his other free time, though, Jerome wrote brilliant but vicious tracts against misguided churchmen. And so when Pope Damasus died in 385, Jerome had to leave Rome to flee his legions of enemies.

It didn't help that Jerome crossed paths with and influenced many of the leading socialites of Rome, who went on to pursue monastic and ascetic practices instead of the party scene. Can you imagine if Paris Hilton and the Kardashians dropped everything one day and decided to become Christian monastics? Well, that was the beautiful havoc Jerome wreaked on the social scene in Rome—to the chagrin of many of the city's powerful figures.

St. Jerome's final stop was in Bethlehem, where he led the life to which he was initially drawn—that of a studious hermit. These last three decades or so were his most productive as he produced many polemical treatises and finished the Vulgate Bible. Even here, though, he wasn't safe from the people he continued to anger with his writings. He once had to flee a mob of Pelagians—a heretical group—who tried to burn down the monastery.

Despite his theological provocations, Jerome died of natural causes in his cell in Bethlehem in the year 420.

What are some of the main lessons and questions we can take away from the life of St. Jerome?

Love for Scripture and Tradition

Jerome carried with him a great love for Scripture that animated his monastic life wherever he went. He also had a great love for the entire apostolic and Catholic tradition that brought him the Gospel of Jesus Christ.

He was the first to translate the Septuagint and the Greek New Testament into the Latin spoken by the average people of the western part of the Roman Empire. In doing so he went not only to the Greek New Testament, but back to the original Hebrew of the Jewish scriptures.

This was not without controversy. The Jewish scriptures of the early Catholic Church were based on the Greek translation found in the Septuagint, and all of the quotes from it in the Greek New Testament came from the Septuagint. In going back to the original Hebrew he was departing from the accepted apostolic tradition of the early Church, and the ordinary practice of most of the Jews in the Roman Empire in the time of Christ. No less than the great St. Augustine, whom we have already considered, debated with St. Jerome over this issue.

The call to translate either language into the vernacular was of huge significance. Jerome's push to use the vernacular was related to his conviction about the importance of reading the Scriptures—how are the people to reap the benefits of the Word of God if they can't understand the language it has been presented in? This was also an act of faith in the people of the early Church, trusting them to read the Scriptures prayerfully and faithfully. We can learn from this and validate St. Jerome's trust by reading the Word regularly and prayerfully!

Let's pause and ask ourselves some questions: What Bible translation do we use? Do we have any interest in the original languages, and how they can help us go deeper along with our modern English or other vernacular translations? Do we see Scripture in the context of the Church from which it was established, or try to interpret it outside of space and time? Do we allow the principles found in Scripture to guide us in our walk with Christ today, under the inspiration of the Holy Spirit and the leadership of the one, holy, Catholic, and apostolic Church?

Holiness and Scripture Study

This leads to our next lesson from St. Jerome. Jerome's monastic lifestyle, as well as his insistence on ascetical holiness for himself and all who followed him, is a powerful lesson for any serious student of Scripture today. Jerome not only studied the Gospel; he lived it in the radical way that had been indicative of the monastic state of life. That is: The Scriptures must be lived or they are powerless.

Do we live the gospel life we study, or do we prefer just to study and talk about it? Are we willing to submit to a time-tested lifestyle of radical gospel living, or do we prefer to do it on our own without any guidance or instruction from those with more experience than ourselves?

God Uses Us Despite Our Personalities

Most commentators are quick to point out that Jerome was an irascible fellow! Despite his obvious desire to serve God without compromise and his great intellect, he was easily drawn into debate. Don't get me wrong; Jesus stirred up a few waves too! But we should avoid them unless necessary.

There are many scriptures encouraging peace. There also many instances of being attacked for following Jesus, who was Himself rejected, persecuted, and crucified by the very people He came to help. St. Paul sums it up simply when he encourages, "If possible, on your part, live at peace with all." (Rom. 12:18) And to his spiritual son, Timothy, he says, "Remind people of these things and charge them before God to stop disputing about words. This serves no useful purpose since it harms those who listen." (2 Tim. 2:14)

No doubt, in the heat of defining doctrine about essential elements of Christian faith and morality the early Church fathers sometimes erred in this regard, and even the most peaceful of them was at times forced into the aggressive defense of the authentic faith. We can easily criticize such apparent intolerance from the safety of over 1500 years of hindsight as we enjoy the doctrinal clarity they established through such sacrifice.

St. Jerome was, even among the often-intense Church fathers, still a bit "hot under the hood." And yet God still used him to be one of the great defenders and definers of orthodoxy in the tumultuous early days of the Church!

How about us? We love Jesus. We want to follow Him without compromise. We might even want to be modern monastics. But we have personality flaws, too! Yet, God still loves us, and uses us for His purposes. It's up to us to cooperate with Him!

There is a difference between our personality and our person. Our person is our entire body, soul, and spirit. Our personality is what we wrap ourselves in to face a very rough and violent world. Our personality acquires and builds up layer after layer of habits and patterns we use to protect ourselves. Our person is the child of God who remains within. The tragedy is when we confuse the personality we acquire for our real person. Scripture calls this the "old self." It is brought to the cross to die with Christ so that our real self can be awakened and reborn in the Spirit through the resurrection of Jesus Christ.

Study Questions

1) Do we use the current translations of Scripture and the liturgy to our full advantage?

2) How well do we handle difficulties in our relationships?

3) Do we see the difference between our personality and our deepest person, and do we allow our truest self in Christ to be awakened and reborn?

St. John Cassian

St. John Cassian is one of the most important figures in the spread of monasticism from Palestine and Egypt to the West. His *Institutes* and *Conferences* are most important in documenting Egyptian monasticism, and are mentioned as fundamental for the serious monastic in the Rule of Benedict. The *Institutes* describe the structure and function of the monasteries of Egypt, and the *Conferences* are one of several compilations of the teachings of the Desert

Fathers. It is from the *Institutes* that we find his list and treatment of the Eight Thoughts.

St. John Cassian's Christian monastic journey began in Romania, then moved to Bethlehem in Palestine, and then through an exercise in providence using disobedience, to Lower Egypt. While he documents the Pachomian monasticism of Upper Egypt, most scholars doubt that he personally visited there; rather, he was describing what he heard from monks in the Lower Desert. He was then asked to found an Egyptian-styled monastery in Marseilles in Southern France.

His adaptation from Evagrius Ponticus of the Eight Thoughts form the foundation from which St. John Climacus in St. Catherine's Monastery in the Sinai and St. Gregory the Great in the West get the well-known Seven Cardinal, or Capital Sins. Personally, I prefer the older eightfold list due to the interconnected psychological processes and spiritual journeys described from one concept to the next. These are most helpful in monastic spiritual direction today, and can be easily adapted for all serious Christians in both the East and West.

Theologically he is often tainted by claims of "semi-Pelagianism"—a theological position situated halfway between the strong emphasis on divine predestination and grace taught by Augustine and the human effort emphasized by the heretic Pelagius. (This criticism has not been as important in the Christian East as in the West.) In any event it is not within our scope to examine his theology, but rather to look at his monastic life and teachings.

The Life

John Cassian was born around the year 360 and educated well in his formative years, owing to the wealth of his parents. He and a friend, Germanus, traveled to Palestine where they joined a monastery near Bethlehem. While they were happy in this life, it was known throughout the Christian world that the greatest and wisest monastics were in the Egyptian deserts—so that's where John Cassian and Germanus set off to.

They were so taken by the incredible lives of the Desert Fathers that they overstayed their leave of absence; despite their intention to be away for only a short while, they only visited Bethlehem once more in their lives. While I would never counsel disobedience, this is an example of God using John Cassian's disobedience to achieve great things! God is even greater than our mistakes and sins!

While John Cassian and Germanus stayed in Egypt the unstable Bishop Theophilus of Alexandria undertook a persecution of Egyptian monks who followed the theologian Origen—which the two friends did. They fled to Constantinople where they met the great St. John Chrysostom, who was Patriarch of Constantinople. When John Chrysostom was exiled at the urging of Theophilus, Cassian and Germanus were sent to Rome to ask for Pope Innocent I's support.

This may seem complicated, but here's the point: A collection of troubling events—John Cassian and Germanus's disobedience and, far more seriously, Theophilus's campaign against the Origenists—brought Cassian to Rome, where he could fulfill his calling: bringing Egyptian monasticism to the West. Providence was at work in ways we can only see in hindsight.

From Rome, John Cassian was sent to southern Gaul, near modern Marseilles, where he founded the first monasteries in Western Europe—one for men and one for women. The organization of these communities influenced the great St. Benedict and through him, as we will see in the next chapter, the entire history of Western Christianity. It was here at Marseilles that Cassian wrote his famous and important *Institutes* and *Conferences*. He died in his monastery around 435.

Institutes and *Conferences*

The *Institutes* are one of the earliest descriptions of cenobitical Egyptian monastic life from the perspective of an observer and are some of the most valuable sources we have for monastic history.

The *Institutes*, along with the *Conferences* of the eremitical Desert Fathers, were commissioned around 420 AD by Bishop Castor of Aptia Julia in Gaul (France) to help establish a cenobitical monastery there based on Egyptian models.

But while his books were written in Latin, they were rather quickly translated into Greek, which indicates the Eastern monks recognized him as one of their own. This is an important point! Though he came from a monastery in Bethlehem and went on to establish monasteries in the West in Southern Gaul, even the monks of Egypt recognize themselves in his descriptions.

The *Institutes* deal with the external organization of monastic communities. What is of interest is the description of things like monastic clothing—at once uniform, symbolic, and practical—and monastic work. While there's nothing too groundbreaking, there are two points of interest to discuss.

First is the monastic habit, or clothing, which is unique to the Egyptian desert. One detail of special interest is the institution of the monastic hood, based on the traditional head gear of infants, worn at all times small and fitted around the face and covering the neck and shoulders. The purpose of this garment is to remind the monks to be childlike. (*Institutes* 3) Another interesting detail is that the clothing of the desert was not strictly applied to the Southern

European monasteries Cassian established since it was too imprac-
tical. So, monastic garb was unique and symbolic, but also adapt-
able to each region for the sake of practicality. (*Institutes* 10)

Second, the *Institutes* also give a description of a monastic office, or
daily prayer ritual, angelically inspired to include at least 12 Psalms
at the major prayer hours. This is interesting because it gives a fuller
description of an office described only generally by earlier sources.
It is an important part of the evolution of all subsequent monastic
expressions, both in the East and in the West.

The *Institutes* go on to describe the balance between work and
prayer, the monks' renunciation of private property, a life of obedience to the leader and the brothers, and the renunciation of food
through discipline of the diet.

As important and interesting as these details of monastic life are,
St. John Cassian's most enduring teachings are his Eight Thoughts.

Eight Thoughts or Vices

Have you ever wondered why we so easily get angry? What about
why we so easily get bitter or bored? And why do we crave attention and quickly feel overlooked, even as we are embarrassed and
frustrated by our growing egotism and pride? The Eight Thoughts
of monastic history show in stunning and sometimes tragically
humorous detail the answers to these questions. They provide an
ancient source for answers to universal psychological and spiritual experiences.

The Eight Thoughts (Greek: λογισμοι, or *logismoi*) are sometimes
called "vices," or even more personalized, "demons." While not
entirely accurate, this does comply with the Egyptian Christian
teaching, based on Scripture, that devils possess the power to

tempt us by placing thoughts into our mind, but that it is up to us to choose to entertain them or not. Cassian did not create this list, but rather inherited and rearranged it from Evagrius, who himself got it from the earlier Greeks. The list is as follows:

- Gluttony

- Sexual Sin

- Avarice

- Anger

- Bitterness

- Boredom

- Self-Glory

- Pride

From these eight all other vices are born. Three lead the way: Gluttony, Avarice, and Self-Glory.

Reflecting on these three vices, we realize that small sins leads to big sins, and when we don't get what we want, we get angry. And when anger is not healed it becomes bitterness and boredom. We end up negative and lethargic. Likewise, from the seemingly harmless desire for attention and legitimate credit, we often end up doubling down on this pattern and giving ourselves over completely to egotism and pride. Then our whole life becomes a downward cycle of misery and loneliness. Let's look at these in a bit of detail.

Gluttony

We think of "gluttony" as eating to extreme excess, but it can also include seemingly harmless choices like eating when not hungry or eating to the point of being "satiated," or what we would call "stuffed." This is a small, almost unnoticeable sin. No one is going to tell us not to have that second helping, or to take smaller portions. We often only notice it through the pounds we slowly put on through the years.

Sexual Sin

This is sometimes called "fornication" and is carnal sin with major consequences. It is not small, unnoticeable, or seemingly harmless. This includes breaking celibacy for monks, or anything outside of Catholic teaching on holy sexual activity, which the Church defines as 1) mutually self-giving, 2) within the context of marriage, and 3) open physically and psychologically to the procreation of new life. God knows we live in a sexually promiscuous culture where self-indulgence is encouraged and praised, and where the divorce of sex from procreation has reestablished a new Sodom and Gomorrah.

Avarice

This includes the desire for physical possessions and wealth, but also includes the desire to control things, situations, or people. You don't need me to tell you that we live in a consumerist culture where we try to fill spiritual needs through earthly possessions. We end up possessed by our possessions, of course, and terribly frustrated, angry, and bitter in a way that leads to discouragement, opens the door for depression, and leaves us feeling helpless. Avarice also has social ramifications, creating a culture where the elite few control the many by buying off the media and politicians as part of a new oligarchy as evil as any from previous eras.

Cassian goes into a tragically humorous story about a monk who starts by keeping just a little wealth—first for the poor, and then for himself in sickness or old age—but he ends up obsessed by his possessions. He then becomes accusatory against his superiors who catch him in his devious schemes. Eventually he leaves the monastery, ending up worse off than when he first accepted Jesus Christ in monastic life. While not always ending up quite so tragic, any monastic leader is well aware of similar stories with failed monastic vocations! There really is nothing new under the sun!

Anger

When you don't get the food you want, the sex you want, or the possessions and control you want, first you get frustrated, and then you get angry. There is such a thing as a valid godly anger, but most of us are destroyed by an ungodly anger that eats us up inside. It also leads to deeper problems. The Fathers mention not only anger with people, but also with inanimate objects. (Do you ever get angry at broken pots, or squeaky doors, and the like? Or how about slow Internet, or dropped cell phone calls?) When anger has taken up residence deep in our soul it only grows and spreads; it needs to be expunged.

Bitterness

This is sometimes called dejection, and with good reason: That's where unhealed anger heads! When anger is not healed it settles deep into the heart in bitterness which poisons every thought, emotion, word, and relationship. Do you find yourself repeating the same patterns of failed relationships or work habits over the years? Soon the glass is always half empty. It makes us negative and miserable, leading to discouragement and depression that can make us feel utterly helpless.

(There are really only two kinds of people: Happy and unhappy. The difference has little to do with whether or not we face success or tragedy. It has everything to do with how we face them. If we face them with a faith that personifies what we hope for in the future— resurrection in Jesus Christ!—in the here and now, we will be happy. If not, no matter how much success we achieve, we will never be truly happy.)

Boredom

When bitterness isn't healed you eventually get bored with everything! This is nothing less than giving up on everything good and beautiful—a resignation to utter helplessness that makes monastic life intolerable. Monastic teachers say at this point the monk tends to drift off into sleep throughout the day, or depart entirely from monastic life. This is called *acidia*, or the noonday devil, for it strikes in the middle of the desert day. To some extent it is unavoidable. Once the novelty of monastic life wears off after a few years, then one's faith is really tested. When the extraordinary is no longer found in the ordinary, then our faith in the extraordinariness of a faith-filled everyday life is put to the test.

This downward trajectory from desire to frustration, from frustration to anger, and from anger to bitterness and boredom is all too familiar to any experienced monastic. Those in monastic leadership see it from the inside as they hear the private conferences of individual members through the weeks, months, years, and even decades of their lives. If this is not healed monasteries become places where individual members learn how to merely coexist with each other without really loving each other in Christ. These places become more like occupied tombs, rather than the empty tombs from which monks have risen to new life in Christ. It is always tragic. The same can happen in parishes, ministries, or even our families. In today's environment of failed relationships, frustrating work patterns, and the resulting discouragement and depression that leads to despair, this is all the more important.

Self-Glorification

This is sometimes called "self-esteem," but in light of the modern, more benign definition of self-esteem I prefer to use "self-glory." And that is what it really means: to claim for yourself what is best left to God. Ironically, it often comes from lacking a true understanding and appreciation for how much God loves us. He creates us and redeems us through the divine rescue of Jesus to the point of giving His own life so that we might live! And He rises up again to manifest the absolute victory of self-giving love over self-obsession.

This is usually manifested in monks becoming petty and self-serving. Always wanting to be praised and appreciated, they are never happy with anyone, for no one fully gratifies the high opinion they have of themselves. It then becomes a kind of feedback loop as they become even more angry, bitter, and bored. This often manifests as an obsessive concern over one's rights or ideological issues and little real concern for the rights and welfare of others in daily life. Again, this is a tragic pattern we see played out not only in monasteries, but also throughout our entire Western culture today.

Pride

Pride ends the list as the final and worst sin, the one the Western tradition calls "the mother of vices." It begins the list in the West's seven capital, or deadly sins. Regardless, it is the end result of the Eight Thoughts, for it means the complete spiritual blindness of the soul, and the culmination of the moral decline of the human person.

There is a logic to the list. The notion is that giving into small, almost unnoticeable indulgences leads to major sin. The need to control everyone and everything leads to frustration and anger, which give way to bitterness and boredom. The desire to glorify yourself beyond a healthy positive self-image as a child of God leads to pride. Both the Western list of capital sins and the Eight Thoughts regard pride as the worst sin, but they get at this idea differently: Whereas the Western "deadly" sins begin with pride, the Eight Thoughts concludes with it as the culmination of vice.

We once had a Benedictine Abbot as our Canonical Visitor from our bishop to our monastic community. He was a good Arkansas boy with a brilliant scholarly command of Scripture and monastic life. He taught us to "chase the rabbit," back to its hole, or follow our thoughts back to their real origin. Where do they come from, and where do they really lead? He taught us to look deeply into the ultimate source and destination of the thoughts that come and go through our minds. Some of these thoughts come from God. Some come from our own creativity. And some come from evil. It's important to know where our thoughts come from—and where they are going—in deciding how to entertain them within our own mind and soul.

Combating the 8 Thoughts or Vices

But there is good news in Christ! The fathers give some cures in Christ that are not only spiritual and emotional, but also practical, powerful, and sometimes downright earthy as well. And as we shall see, most of this is not rocket science. There are no deep mystical and mysterious ways to cure them. Most of this is very simple, practical, and applicable to all people.

Gluttony

Gluttony can be cured by moderate fasting. This means eating once or twice a day in modest amounts. The fathers say that extreme fasting leads to over eating after the fast. Surely some of us relate to that pattern of fad dieting? So, their cure is neither magical, mystical, nor faddish. Rather it is extremely pastoral, practical, and doable for the average Christian. For me, this means eating good wholesome food every day, but trying to keep my caloric intake around 1500 a day. Once every week or so I have something a little special. I enjoy good food just like most folks, but I find that I just feel better when not carrying around the extra body bulk. Then I have greater energy to devote to spiritual things so I can soar to the heavens even while having both feet planted firmly on the ground. Everything in our lives is connected!

Sexual Sin

Again, the fathers are eminently practical. Since most sexual sin occurred at night, they emphasize a good, even exhausting day's work before going to bed. Nothing magic about that. You're just too tired to fool around! They also recommend getting up in the middle of the night to pray if one is tempted.

Today we could easily add that, since we become what we habitually think, control of our use of social media and the Internet, not to mention TV, is most important in avoiding sexual sin. Addiction to pornography is becoming more common, even among devoutly religious people. Clerics and monastics are not immune!

I would add that, in combatting sexual sin, there's nothing more important than using all of the spiritual tools at our disposal to enter into a personal relationship of love with Jesus Christ, who is our primary Spouse. This is especially true for me in my use of charismatic gifts of the Spirit to energize my spiritual relationship with Jesus Christ. We fight fire with fire! We stir up the power of the Spirit to overcome the power of sin. When this is fulfilled, I am less tempted to look for carnal or other earthly means for satisfying my inner need for intimacy that can only be fulfilled spiritually. I am aflame with the Spirit of God!

Avarice

Again, no magic tricks here! The fathers recommend living a simple monastic community life in obedience to an established rule and superior. There is nothing better for the curbing of our need to control than learning how to really listen to a religious superior, not to mention our brothers and sisters in community, and to relinquish our personal possessions. For the rest of us this is also twofold: First, just get rid of your unnecessary stuff! Second, learn how to listen in obedience to parents and siblings in the community of the domestic church, not to mention in the community of your local church or ministry, and even in the secular workplace. The first is tough, but relatively simple. The second is tougher, and takes a lifetime! If you don't learn this obedience and mutual self-reliance, community, or family itself, becomes impossible, and we are forced to move back into an illusory individualism that promises something it can never deliver. As Jackson Browne sings in one of his songs, "No matter how far I run, I just can't seem to get away from me." Living intentional community life—whether in a monastery or a suburban home—will cure you of this avarice quickly.

Anger

Anger is cured by forgiveness. This may seem simple, but it's never easy. Forgiveness is not a feeling that magically happens to us. It's a decision we make that stirs up and directs our feelings. Yet, when we think about it it's really far easier to forgive than to carry around judgment. When we judge we bind others through negative attitudes that cripple relationships—and we also bind and cripple ourselves. When we forgive we bind evil, but loose righteousness. Binding and loosing is not just for Church leadership with Popes and bishops. It is also for all of us.

It's said of St. Francis that he taught leaders that there is no sinner anywhere in the world who should not be called back to forgiveness simply by looking into his or her spiritual leader's eyes! They must look at others the way God looks at us, seeing what God sees and forgiving as God forgives. That's a tall order! This does not condone sin, but exactly the opposite; it attracts and calls to repentance through both truth and great love. Truth alone can be hard. Love alone can be aimless. We need both to get us to our destination in Christ. It doesn't enable negative behavior, but empowers positive changes in behavior.

Bitterness

We overcome bitterness by choosing the good things of God daily: virtue over vice, beauty over ugliness. There are two kinds of people: winners and losers; the successful and the unsuccessful. It has little to do with how much money we make, or whether or not we face challenges and tragedies. We all do that. It has everything to do with how we face tragedy! We can face our tragedies, both big and small, with faith and turn them into triumphs, or we can face them with doubt and let them make us bitter. Then bitterness poisons our whole life. Plus, "like attracts like." Positive people attract positive people and empower negative people to change. Negative people attract negative people and poison the positive things left in their life.

Boredom

The monastic fathers say that if you are bored, get up and do some-thing positive for God and for others! It's a deceptively simple solu-tion; the difficulty with boredom is that nothing feels worth doing. It takes an act of the will to overcome that and rediscover the enjoy-ment of living life. This stirs up and redirects emotions in a positive way that empowers the positive, rather than enabling the negative. You'll soon discover there aren't enough hours in the day for all the wonderful things you can do in and for Christ every single day of your life! Obstacles become challenges! And insecurities become adventures! Life will never again be boring or dull.

Self-Glory

The cure for self-glory is also simple: Give all glory to Jesus Christ! St. Francis used to internally give all praise and glory to Jesus every time he was complimented or praised. We can also do this when we are persecuted. The use of the charismatic gifts of praise and wor-ship are invaluable here as well. When we want to hold on to praise and glory, or seek them when others get them and we don't, the supernatural energy of the Spirit enables us to "let go and let God" by giving Him everything! Suddenly we are more concerned about the gifts of God and the gifts of others than we are about being noticed for our own gifts. Then we are fulfilled by being completely focused on giving to God and others. And that is the greatest gift!

Pride

This is more intense, and requires intense measures. The fathers recommend meditation on the suffering and humiliation of Jesus in the Passion and on the cross to cure our pride. This should be graphic. It is also sometimes prolonged. We see every wound, and every drop of blood shred out of love for the Father, and for us! That Jesus would go through this for each one of us personally is enough to bring anyone to his knees in humble appreciation, reverence, and prayer. How can we not weep in the face of being loved so much by God in Jesus?

Context

Before we leave our treatment of John Cassian and the Eight Thoughts, it would be good to place them in the context of the overall spiritual journey taught by the eastern Christian monastic fathers.

We are supposed to read and consider the Eight Thoughts in the context of *hesychia* (Greek ἡσύχιος), or Sacred Stillness. Here we quiet the body through appropriate asceticism and discipline. This includes a calm and quiet posture, and controlled use of the breath united with the name of Jesus. Then the emotions and thoughts settle down, and can be properly focused. The human spirit is ready to burn again through the Spirit of God.

This has been compared to calming the waters of a pond so we might properly reflect an image; the muddy waters of turbulence come clear through stillness. It is in this state that we can see what is really happening in the pond of our soul through Watchfulness (Greek νεπσις, nepsis), and can discern the movement of God (and the Devil) through the Eight Thoughts. This Watchfulness is neither anxious nor obsessive. It is filled with peace and perseverance in the grace that Jesus gives through the Spirit. We can then apply the proper cures in Christ. We will discuss this further in the chapter on Eastern Monasticism.

This leads us on a journey not unlike those described in various traditional texts in Western Christian spirituality. Without getting into the weeds of these classifications, the Christian East sometimes describes a threefold journey in which the Intuitive, or emotional, Rational, or mental, and Intellective, or contemplative faculties of the human soul are redirected and properly ordered in Christ. This is not unlike the Western classifications of the Purgative, Illuminative, and Unitive stages of Christianity. It also correlates more or less with the traditional monastic stages of 1) *Lectio Divina*, or sacred reading using Scripture or another sacred text, 2) *Meditatio*, or meditation through the use the imagination and visualization of what we read, 3) *Oratio*, or prayer that stirs the soul in the reality of what we see in the mind, and 4) *Contemplatio*, or contemplation beyond all images or forms in pure intuitive and ecstatic union of spirit in the Holy Spirit with God. These descriptions of this spiritual experience differ in the naming and some of the content of the stages of prayer, but they overlap in trying to describe a familiar mystical journey that is common to all who seriously seek to follow Jesus Christ.

This is a fast 'fly over' description of Christian spiritual life that is too complex for us to go into here. But I mention it to pique interest in those seeking to know more. This monastic journey is not just for monastics, but also for all Christians. I recommend further prayer and study of the entire context of this spiritual journey to any serious follower of Jesus.

Study Questions

1) Do we see how God can use even the mistakes in our life to accomplish a greater good when we walk with repentance, forgiveness, and faith from our past?

2) Do we have an order, or a rule of life based on the teaching of the Church and the saints, to help guide us through daily life?

3) Can we see the interconnection among the Eight Thoughts, and all the vices and virtues? Do we pursue the source of our thoughts, as well as their final end?

4) Do we apply cures in Christ that are simple, time tested, and reliable, or do we try to reinvent the wheel as we face each challenge?

5) Do we see the greater spiritual journey through the stages of spiritual life, or are we fixated on one aspect of spirituality without growing into others?

CHAPTER 7: ST. BENEDICT, BALANCE, AND MODERATION

Do we ever find our life out of balance? St. Benedict brings balance and moderation to our entire way of life so that we might prosper once more in Christ and the Church!

I remember with fondness my first experience in a Benedictine Abbey. I was going to visit a good friend of my Franciscan spiritual father at Abbey Press at Saint Meinrad Archabbey in southern Indiana about handling a new idea for my first musical setting for the Mass. This setting, called "The Lord's Supper," was eventually released by Sparrow records and went on to be quite successful!

I was stunned to reverence by the almost medieval image of the Archabbey nestled in the rolling hills of the Midwest close to the Ohio River. After meeting my friend he ushered me into the gorgeous church where the monastic office was sung in stunning simplicity and beauty. I was thoroughly and completely mesmerized in the Spirit.

I also shared my first monastic meal with the monks in the huge refectory. Perhaps it was because this was my first such experience, but the refectory seemed truly larger than life! I was amazed at the table reading in silence, and then at the recreation afterwards which took place in the thoroughly family-like setting that is typical of Benedictine hospitality.

It was during that meal that I met Fr. Columba Stewart, internationally known as an expert on monastic liturgy and chant. Little did I know I was sitting across from one of the most celebrated monastics in the world! And little did he know that the musical setting we were discussing would become such an overnight success in the near future. I found him immensely knowledgeable and experienced, accompanied by typical Benedictine humility. I was deeply impressed, and will never forget the encounter.

I also went to the little shrine of Monte Cassino in the woods a short walk from the main abbey complex. I must confess that it was here that the Lord spoke to me in powerful ways that defy what I can describe in words. These little words of grace were part of the foundation of my own monastic calling. Today I call upon Benedict and Scholastica, along with Francis and Clare, Pachomius and Antony, Romuald and Bruno as monastic patrons and patronesses of our new integrated monastic community in the Brothers and Sisters of Charity.

The Life

St. Benedict was born around the year 480 in Norcia, or Nursia (Umbria, Italy). He died at his monastery of Monte Cassino on March 21, 543. What happened in between would help shape Western Europe, the entire Roman Catholic Church, and beyond.

The Rule that bears Benedict's name, and that established a distinct Western monasticism, continues to bear fruit to this day. Here's just a brief rundown of Benedict's influence and impact not just on the Church but on human civilization, some of which will be discussed at greater length later in this book:

- The Benedictine monk Augustine of Canterbury evangelized Britain, and the Benedictine-educated Boniface evangelized Germany.

- The Celts used his rule of life in their unique integrated take on monasticism as it spread through continental Europe.

- The great Benedictine monastery at Cluny shaped religious life and spread Christianity throughout Europe in the 9th and 10th centuries.

- St. Bernard of Clairvaux, widely regarded as the most influential and most respected man in Europe during his lifetime, was involved in the Cistercian Benedictine reform of the 11th century.

- Benedictines were many of the great scientists and thinkers of the Middle Ages; they made huge scientific and theological advances with innovations as basic as the modern plough for agriculture. They also maintained European civilization through the Black Death.

- More recently, the Benedictine reform at Solesmes in France has brought forth a revival of Gregorian chant that has blessed the world with beautiful music, including best-selling recordings from Santa Domingo in Spain.

- The Benedictines were some of the most active Catholics in early America, setting up centers of education based on Benedictine standards whose graduates continue to shape our nation.

For me, Benedict is the master of balance and moderation. He takes the various monastic streams of the past—sometimes extreme in their ways of life—and makes them eminently livable for the average man or woman who wanted to seek a more radical embrace of the Gospel of Jesus Christ. This is the same message Benedict gives monastics of later ages, and of our own time. It is his singular genius.

The only ancient biography of the saint comes from *The Life and Miracles of St. Benedict* in the *Dialogues* of St. Gregory the Great. Beyond this typical hagiography, or legendary life and miracles of a saint, the Church of his own day is virtually silent. It is only later generations that produce greater commentaries confirming his Life. The Life is filled not only with the story of his founding of monasteries, but with numerous miracle stories that flesh out the directives of the Rule with the daily lives of Benedict and his monks.

Born in Norcia in the beautiful Umbrian countryside of Italy, he was sent to Rome to be educated as a master of rhetoric. After becoming disillusioned with the worldliness he saw in the civil culture and the church in Rome, Benedict left his schooling and retired to a cave as a lay hermit. His solitude, reminiscent of the Desert Fathers, was so complete that a kindly monk named Romanus from a nearby monastery, who was bringing supplies and checking on him regularly, had to remind him of the proper date for Easter. He encouraged him to break his fast and feast a little on the greatest day of the year!

Benedict's holiness became well-known after some shepherds stumbled upon him and thought at first that he was an animal. Realizing he was just an unkempt hermit, they spread the word and he became something of a local celebrity. But all was not easy for the young hermit monk—far from it! Benedict was eventually tempted sorely by all the traditional tricks of the Devil that play with a young monk's heart and mind, especially the temptation of lust. Like a true spiritual warrior, he overcame these in and through Jesus Christ. Once he had surmounted these challenges in solitude he was ready to emerge from his cave and minister the good news of Christ to others. And it happened soon and in a way he did not expect.

When the local monastery of Vicavaro lost its abbot, they decided that the nearby hermit was an ideal candidate for the vacancy. Benedict, of course, declined. But they doggedly persisted. Perhaps they thought an abbot of growing fame would be a boon for their monastery? But they were in for a surprise! Once he accepted the role, his rule of self-sacrifice and prayer was far too stringent for these rather lax monks—so they tried to kill him! This was not an uncommon pattern with reforming abbots perceived as overly strict. (Nowadays, we just vote them out!) He was miraculously saved by the breaking of his cup of poisoned wine. In response, he simply returned to solitude at Subiaco, but he quickly attracted disciples. He then founded a new monastery under his discipline, and the famous Rule of Benedict developed through his practical experience. He had moved from the life of a hermit to the life of a founder and abbot of a cenobitical monastery. But he never lost the love for eremitical solitude, and allowed for it in his Rule.

At Subiaco the first monastery developed and grew. The life of the monks was orderly and successful. They grew in holiness individually and communally, and reached out to those in need through miracles and simple ministries. It was a thoroughly balanced life. The miracles that emerge from lives fully converted to Jesus Christ and empowered by the Spirit of God abounded!

But such a life is not without resistance, persecution, and trial. Benedict and his disciples were no exception. A local parish priest named Florentius became very jealous of the success of Benedict and his monastery. We can imagine his thoughts and words. "Who are these laymen? Where did they get their holiness? Where did Benedict go to seminary? Where did he get his training? Why are local folks flocking to them and not to me?" And so it went.

The poor priest devised an unholy plan. First he sought to discredit Benedict's monks by starting rumors and creating gossip. But it didn't work; he was simply ignored by the townsfolk and by the humble Benedict. Next, he even tried to murder Benedict by sending him poisoned bread. But that didn't work. Benedict's pet raven took the poisonous bread away, and the dreadful plot was exposed through the Spirit. Meanwhile the monks steadily grew in holiness. So, the exasperated priest finally hired seven prostitutes and sent them to dance naked in the cloister of the monks to entice them to sin.

Well, that didn't work either! The same Benedict that was first tempted in solitude as a hermit was not tempted in the least, and simply sent the ladies away. But he worried about his young and inexperienced monks. After much prayer for discernment he decided to take his monks and depart to another place. The priest watched gleefully from a balcony as the monks departed. He was sure he had succeeded. But all was not as it seemed. The balcony from which he watched collapsed under the poor parish priest, killing him. Whoa! That seemed like divine retribution to the young monks, who rejoiced at the report that Benedict had proven victorious. But Benedict did not rejoice. He wept, mourning that the priest had died unconverted and that the young monks rejoiced in victory, which betrayed their worldly outlook.

Grappling with these concerns, Benedict had prayed and discerned to move on to another place. He stayed with the plan. He settled the entire community at Monte Cassino, the site of an old pagan shrine, and baptized it through the holiness of pure monastic living. This monastery prospered and started daughter houses all living under the moderate Rule of Benedict.

Towards the end of Benedict's life God showed him a terrible vision in a dream: the destruction of Monte Cassino by invading barbarians. In fact this did end up happening 30 years after his death when the Lombards invaded in 543. Monte Cassino and Tarrecino, another monastery founded by Benedict, were sacked, and his monks fled for refuge in the city of Rome. In this Benedict was aware that all we build on earth, even monasteries and church buildings, will collapse and fall. Only Jesus and the Church remain forever. Only spiritual realities and true relationships in gospel communities and ministries last. All else can, and often does, crumble and fall. This is humbling, but reassuring at the same time. All the great saints know it well.

Before Benedict's death we know that he granted his twin sister, Scholastica, the grace of sharing a simple meal with him. She had also given her life to God in a female expression of the monastic movement started by Benedict. She was in fact the abbess of her own monastery, and she wanted to share some quality time with her twin brother. Benedict went to her monastic convent, which by the customs of the time she was not permitted to leave, and at the close of the meal he prepared to leave and go back to his monastery, since staying overnight was considered improper. By providence she knew it would be their last time to meet on earth, and tried to convince him to stay the night, but he refused. But God had other plans! Suddenly a torrential storm descended upon the convent which prevented Benedict from departing for his monastery. So he had to stay the night in a guest cell at Scholastica's monastery. What a monk could not grant, a saintly nun received by going directly to God! What was denied an abbot, was granted to an abbess. What a monastic father was denied was given to a monastic mother by God the Father.

Not long after this St. Scholastica departed this life, and Benedict saw her saintly soul ascend to heaven. He delighted in her final victory, and soon followed her in his own departure to obtain his eternal reward for a life of saintly holiness and astounding achievements for Christ, the Church, and the monastic way of life. He left us a brilliant Rule that made monasticism something the average person could follow without either excess or laxity, but in balance and moderation.

Study Questions

1) Do we find imbalance in our life? Are our lifestyle habits sometimes immoderate?

2) Do we find our secular life unfulfilling, or downright disgusting? Are we willing to step out of it to discover a deeper calling and vocation in Christ and the Church?

3) Do we find a balance between solitude and community? Are we willing to be tested by retreats into solitude before we try to minister with and to others?

4) How well do we face resistance in the Church?

5) Do we always live by the letter of the law, or are we willing to live by the grace of the highest law of love in appropriate ways?

6) Do we sometimes feel that our accomplishments will come to little or nothing for later generations? Are we willing to let God build the spiritual house in His way so that real resurrection in Christ can amaze us?

St. Benedict, Moderation, and Balance: Part II

Now that we have looked at St. Benedict's life, let's take a look at some of the high points of his Rule. I have written a book of reflections on the Rule called *The Blessings of St. Benedict*, so I will focus here only on the spiritual heart of the Rule.

I love the Prologue because it sets the tone of the entire Rule. It is based not on legislation, but on an obedience that requires a complete change of lifestyle from one of constant chatter in our mind and with our lips to a contemplative listening that revolutionizes our entire life in Christ.

> Listen carefully, my son, to the master's instructions, and attend to them with the ear of your heart. This is advice from a father who loves you; welcome it, and faithfully put it into practice. The labor of obedience will bring you back to him from whom you had drifted through the sloth of disobedience. This message of mine is for you, then, if you are ready to give up your own will, once and for all, and armed with the strong and noble weapons of obedience to do battle for the true King, Christ the Lord. (RB, Prologue 1:1-2)

The Prologue begins with the exhortation: "Listen my son to a father's instruction, from a father who loves you." In monastic spirituality obedience is rooted in the Latin word which means "to listen." First, do we really listen to God, our leaders in the Church and our community, and our brothers and sisters in Christ when they speak? More often than not we begin putting together our response or reaction before they've even finished speaking!

Monastic obedience encourages an inner stillness that really allows us to listen to what a person has to say. Sometimes they don't express themselves well, so we have to discern what they're really trying to communicate. Sometimes they don't even know themselves very well, so the words only clumsily express their inner spirit. We have to be still in the Spirit of Christ before we can really hear the spirit of another person. Often, it is in listening in docility that we can call it forth from others.

But monastic obedience is far from passive! There are many examples of monks having a prompt, ready, and willing obedience as soon as they hear instructions from God through their leaders, or through their brothers and sisters. Perhaps, the most common story is about the brother who was writing and put down his pen mid-sentence as he heard his elder's command. He made neither excuses nor delay. He didn't say what many of us would: "As soon as I'm finished with this I'll get right to it!" Of course, we remember the biblical example of would-be disciples making excuses about caring for their parents or having just been married for not fully following Christ. These are, of course, valid reasons in themselves, but when used as an excuse for not really following Jesus, they become obstacles to salvation. Obedience is radical stuff! It involves not only passive listening, but also active participation that changes our life for the better.

Self-Will

Benedict continues his teaching on obedience in the Prologue by encouraging monks to be "willing and ready to give up your self-will, once and for all!" The Rule speaks of "self-will" throughout. The Scriptures in a similar way speak of the "old self." Baptismal spirituality is about bringing the old self to the cross to die with Christ as we go under the water, and to rise up as a new creation in Christ as we come out of the water. Benedictine spirituality is saying the same thing regarding "self-will."

I teach that we have settled for a version of ourselves that is incomplete, if not altogether wrong or sinful. This brings us frustration and unhappiness. It is only when we bring the old incomplete self to the cross of Jesus Christ and let it die that we are really able to be raised up a new creation in Christ as the person God originally intended us to be. When viewed this way, such a relinquishing of the old self, or self-will, doesn't sound so bad. In fact it is downright appealing! In this light monastic obedience becomes attractive—something we actually desire, no matter how hard the struggle might seem at times. It is a discipline that leads to spiritual mastery in Christ, Who is the Master!

This is powerful! If we are ready to give up our self-will then obedience becomes easy and liberating. If we still hold on to our self-will, or old self, then obedience under a leader or with others in community becomes intolerable.

Prayer and Grace

> First of all, every time you begin a good work, you must pray to him most earnestly to bring it to perfection. (RB, Prologue 1:4)

Benedict also teaches that before we begin any good work we must pray for the assistance of God's grace. Grace, faith, and works are intimately related. If we try to work without grace our work will not be as fruitful as it could be, and will burn us out in the process. Conversely, if all we do is pray and never work, our prayer will become stagnant and self-serving.

But even prayer is fruitless without the grace of God. That's why at the beginning of monastic common prayer—what today we call the Liturgy of Hours—we say, "O God, come to my assistance. O Lord, make haste to help me." This is an ancient monastic custom going back to the *Institutes* of St. John Cassian well before St. Benedict of Nursia.

And this is most scriptural! Before the apostles could be sent forth to evangelize the world with the Gospel of Jesus Christ they had to wait in Jerusalem for "the power from on high," or the Holy Spirit.

Without the empowerment of the Holy Spirit even the apostles who had lived with Jesus could not fulfill their ministry. Nor can we fulfill ours without the grace of prayer.

School of the Lord's Service

Benedict concludes his Prologue with a self-depreciating comment, along with an encouragement to others. He basically says that all he is trying to do is establish a little "school of the service of the Lord." He says the Rule has established nothing difficult. But he goes on to say that if anything does seem a little harsh or constricting not to immediately depart.

> Therefore we intend to establish a school for the Lord's service. In drawing up its regulations, we hope to set down nothing harsh, nothing burdensome. The good of all concerned, however, may prompt us to a little strictness in order to amend faults and to safeguard love. Do not be daunted immediately by fear and run away from the road that leads to salvation. It is bound to be narrow at the outset. But as we progress in this way of life and in faith, we shall run on the path of God's commandments, our hearts overflowing with the inexpressible delight of love. (RB, Prologue 1: 45-49)

In community we must establish common rules so that we can do essential things together. We must establish set times for prayer, meals, and work. On our own, we might desire to do these things at different times. But we sacrifice our own self-will in order to accomplish the good of the community in and through which we serve Christ. If we are unable to make this sacrifice then living in community becomes impossible, and we will be tempted to depart. Benedict encourages us not to do so, but to stay, sacrifice our own self-will, and find a way in Christ with deeper roots that will permit us to reach much higher than we can ever do on our own.

Chapter 1: Kinds of Monks

> There are clearly four kinds of monks. First, there are the cenobites, that is to say, those who belong to a monastery, where they serve under a rule and an abbot. Second, there are the anchorites or hermits, who have come through the test of living in a monastery for a long time, and have passed beyond the first fervor of monastic life. Thanks to the help and guidance of many, they are now trained to fight against the devil. They have built up their strength and go from the battle line in the ranks of their brothers to the single combat of the desert. Self-reliant now, without the support of another, they are ready with God's help to grapple single-handed with the vices of body and mind. ... Let us pass them by, then, and with the help of the Lord, proceed to draw up a plan for the strong kind, the cenobites. (RB 1: 1-5, 13)

The Rule of Benedict continues the tradition of John Cassian, describing different kinds of monks—two good, and two bad.

The good are: hermits, who live alone after having been tested in obedience; and cenobites who live in community under a rule and abbot. He describes cenobitism as the time-tested and surest way.

He then rather humorously describes the two bad kinds of monks. First are Sarabites, who form monastic groups but who fail to overcome their self-will. And second are Gyrovagues, who are similarly undisciplined wanderers from monastery to monastery—in other words, monastic mooches!

Of Sarabites he says:

> Third, there are the sarabaites, the most detestable kind of monks, who with no experience to guide them, no rule to try them *as gold is tried in a furnace* (Prov. 27:21), have a character as soft as lead. Still loyal to the world by their actions, they clearly lie to God by their tonsure. Two or three together, or even alone, without a shepherd, they pen themselves up in their own sheepfolds, not the Lord's. Their law is what they like to do, whatever strikes their fancy. Anything they believe in and choose, they call holy; anything they dislike, they consider forbidden. (RB 1:6-9)

Of Gyrovagues he goes further:

> Fourth and finally, there are the monks called gyrovagues, who spend their entire lives drifting from region to region, staying as guests for three or four days in different monasteries. Always on the move, they never settle down, and are slaves to their own wills and gross appetites. In every way they are worse than sarabaites... It is better to keep silent than to speak of all these and their disgraceful way of life. (RB 1:10-12)

What do these four kinds of monks have to say to us today? Regarding the two good kinds, we learn that there are different ways to live the monastic life. One size does not fit all. We also learn that training and discipline under an abbot and a community rule is necessary to prepare the average person for authentic solitude in Christ. Those who are unprepared will usually lose the vocation they think they have once they discover the fierce and frightening spiritual warfare common to the hermit's life. It is only through a firm grounding in Christ, the Church, and community that most can succeed in the solitary life of a Christian hermit.

But it is from the bad kind who reject this time-tested pattern that we learn the most. Sarabites teach us that those who refuse to submit to the guidance of an elder and insist on creating their own little group end up considering themselves superior to others, or breaking off from the main group altogether. It is good to know that the concept of "heresy" in Scripture (Titus 3:10–αἱρετικός, *hairetikos*) isn't about healthy diversity of opinion but rather the dangerous division caused by teachings different from the ones passed on through the apostles and their successors—teachings that are specifically held on to with a belligerent stubbornness based on self-will. The same is true in spiritual movements in the Church—some are faithful and foster unity, and others are heretical and foster division. And we still see many divisive groups come and go in modern monasticism.

These are not the same as authentic new monastic communities and movements raised up by the Holy Spirit in union with the Church. The teaching of the Church is clear that the Holy Spirit raises spiritually powerful communities in each era of the Church. But they are always humble, and fully appreciative of the entire monastic tradition that has come before.

There are also modern Gyrovagues! We know all too well of countless individuals that bounce from one movement to the next, and even from one church to the next in a constant search for an elusive perfection. These are folks foolishly addicted to novelty. They are always in search of the "next big thing" in spiritual life. Always searching, they never really find. But the Church is filled with fallible people who are used by a perfect God to accomplish his perfect will. Benedict is clear that it is only by blooming where we are planted, even amidst the imperfections of the Church and the movements within her that we will discover real growth towards perfection (Mt. 5:48–τέλειος, *teleios*) in our own spiritual life.

(There are authentic traveling, or mendicant monastics: the friars and pilgrims of the West, and the hermit "grazers" of Egypt. But they always live in humble obedience to the Church and a monastic discipline that brings stability and peace to themselves and everyone they meet.)

Later Western and early Eastern monastic tradition expound on the two good types on Benedict's list and agree on three essential kinds of monks: 1) cenobites who live in strict community, 2) semi-eremites who live in colonies in lavras or sketes, and 3) hermits and recluses who live alone, attached either to cenobitical communities or to semi-eremitical colonies.

The fact is there is a bit of all these in each of us! We all want solitude and community. We also like to get our own way and to hang out with groups who agree with our religious idiosyncrasies. We also search for spiritual perfection, or sometimes fall into an unhealthy desire for novelty in the Church, our marriage, or our spiritual life. Once we own these tendencies, we can discover the good and use it for the very best for others and ourselves in Christ!

The Rule is far too long to address in this format. Let me humbly suggest reading my book, *The Blessings of St. Benedict,* to get you started on a monastic journey that will take a lifetime to complete. And the journey will be wonderful! I know it has been in my life.

For now let's at least skim across the vast spiritual and pastoral ocean of Benedict's thinking with some of the major points of his Rule.

Chapter 2: The Abbot

There are often great misunderstandings of what proper and balanced obedience to a leader actually means. The Rule gives us some great general guidelines that can help us avoid these. The first regards the role of the Abbot, or spiritual father.

Word and example

The abbot is the spiritual father of the entire monastic community. He stands in the place of Christ, but his rule is not absolute. He must himself abide by certain governing principles. The first is that he is to rule not only by his word, but also by his example. Words are cheap if they aren't backed up by the authority of a truly changed life in Christ. The abbot will only be successful if his life speaks louder than his words.

Spiritual and temporal

As a leader of each local community, the abbot must not only rule spiritually, but also temporally—that is, over the earthly day-to-day functioning of the monastery and the people who inhabit it. In doing this, the spiritual must always take precedence; without adequate time and energy given to the spiritual aspect of leadership, the rest will suffer.

Moderate, adaptable

The abbot must be moderate in his teaching, and be able to adapt the specifics of these teachings to each brother or sister. To some he will be stern, to others he will be gentle and tender. If you are too stern with the meek, they can break. If too gentle and tender with the stubborn and arrogant, they will never listen. The good abbot knows the difference.

Love brothers, hate sins

He must know how to "hate the sin, and love the sinner." This is a cliché, to be sure, but it is full of meaning. It is precisely by hating sin, which separates us from God and is truly bad for us, that we love the sinner. An abbot who confuses these two concepts will either tacitly approve mortal errors, or will isolate himself from his brothers.

Loved not feared

In the end the abbot must be more loved than feared. In the time of Benedict it was expected that leaders in all walks of life establish a baseline of respect through fear. Benedict's teaching, then, was actually quite counter-cultural. Fear must move on to love for, and Scripture says, "Perfect love casts out all fear." (1 Jn. 4:18)

Chapter 3: Counsel And Mutual Obedience

Even the abbot cannot rule autocratically—that is, all by himself. This chapter emphasizes that there is wisdom in the counsel of many. So there are advisory councils that are formed from and work in the community. There is, for instance, a council of seniors and administrators of various departments in the monastery who assist the abbot in smaller day-to-day operations.

Most importantly, though, there is a committee of all monastic members who advise him in making more serious decisions that affect the fate of all in major ways. It is in this latter context that Benedict gives us the brilliant teaching that God's will is sometimes best expressed through even the youngest member of the monastery. So, even the youngest member must be heard, listened to, and reverenced as a mouthpiece for the Spirit of God.

In general we are taught to honor seniors, and love juniors.

Chapter 4: Tools for Good Works

This chapter is often a bit baffling. It is made up of an apparently dis-connected collection of scriptures about good works. But, as with all else in the Rule, there is a logic to it. It moves generally from the external to the internal, and then back to the external. This reminds us of the connection between our internal, prayerful disposition and the effectiveness of our good works. Plus, the entire collec-tion revolves around Jesus' great Sermon on the Mount. Once we understand this essential connection between our prayer life, our works, and Scripture, it can be transformational to our entire life.

It is in this context that we learn how the great teaching of St. Jerome that "ignorance of scripture is ignorance of Christ" is fleshed out in the monastic context. All of this is based on the great teaching that we are to "prefer nothing to Christ." The Benedictine monastic life is entirely Christocentric.

Chapter 5: Obedience

Benedictine obedience means both listening and prompt action. Most folks don't adequately listen before they react. We must listen, however, so that we might wisely respond. But we also must act or listening is in vain.

Our action must be prompt and without resistance. Again, this takes trust in God, who works through the abbot and leaders despite their human shortcomings. We obey not so much the man or woman in leadership, but God who leads us through the leader-ship He has established.

The Rule gives us a stunning teaching about obedience even in seemingly impossible assignments. We are allowed to make a humble representation of our opinion that we are incapable of fulfilling the task. This is done with gentle dialogue, not obstinate debate. We share rather than argue. But if the superior asks to follow the command anyway we are to trust in God's power, not our own, and do the very best we can while asking for God's grace.

Furthermore, we are to fulfill the task without moaning or grumbling. If we complain the benefits of obedience are lost, even though we might physically fulfill the task. Subservience to the will of God is the point of obedience, not any particular piece of work or study.

Defending another

Lastly, we are not to defend another who is being disciplined by appropriate leadership. There is a proper order to be kept in community. We must trust that the leaders of these individuals know more about the situation on the pastoral level then we do.

It might be appropriate to add that in later centuries the Benedictines, and all monastic and consecrated communities of the Church, have incorporated further checks and balances that protect individuals from abusive leadership. But this is never done in a way that leads to disrespect of leadership offices or that even inadvertently leads to anarchy and confusion.

Chapter 6: Silence and Speech

Interestingly, monasteries are not places where monks take vows of silence. I know of no monasteries where such a vow exists. But there are places and times of silence, and an attitude of silence permeates daily life. We are reminded of the scriptural teaching that "in the multitude of words, there lacks not sin." So we are encouraged to silence all evil speech, of course, but even some otherwise good speech that is unnecessary.

This is a tall order! We tend to want to express ourselves all the time and in every situation. Sometimes we think that if we are not talking, God is not speaking! But as the wisdom literature teaches us about the dangers of constant speaking, it will not make us burst to be quiet for a while. We remember the example of the Desert Father, Abba Pambo, who kept a pebble in his mouth for three years to learn the discipline of silence. But nothing quite so harsh is asked of us!

Even though there is only a general attitude of silence that fills the monastery, there are still times and places for strict silence. We are strictly silent after Compline, or Night Prayer. (RB 42) We are also silent in and around the Oratory, or monastery church. (RB 52)

Chapter 7: Humility

The saints teach us that "humility is just the truth"! And St. Francis says, "What we are before God, that we are and nothing more"! James 4:6-10 says that humility is *tapeinos* (ταπεινός), or being brought low to the earth. Our old self is brought low and buried in the grave, so a new person can rise up in Christ! This is the truth of truths.

Benedict gives us a kind of '12 step program' for humility. It is simple, but challenging to the core!

12 Steps

1) Fear, awe and wonder before God.

2) Letting go the old self-will.

3) Obedience to an abbot.

4) Obedience with joy even in difficult things.

5) Voluntary revelation of one's thoughts to a trusted abbot (not just sins as in sacramental confession).

6) Being content with lowliness and poverty in Christ.

7) Finding joy in the gifts of others before having our own gifts noticed and rewarded.

8) Doing only what is part of the common life of the monks and superiors of our monastery.

9) Sacred silence.

10) Refraining from unhealthy laughter.

11) Speaking gently.

12) Being humble as a second nature, held as a light burden in Christ, in every aspect of our life.

We begin with the fear of God, but end in a perfect love that casts out all fear. We begin with discipline in specific things, but end in liberating freedom in all things. We begin with some hard work and even some sorrow, but end in the ease of perfect joy!

Stability in an Unstable World

> Never swerving from his instructions, then, but faithfully
> observing his teaching in the monastery until death, we
> shall through patience share in the sufferings of Christ
> that we may deserve also to share in his kingdom. Amen.
> (RB Prologue, 50)

Let's end this chapter with a look at Benedictine stability. As we
have seen, many monks prior to St. Benedict were holy pilgrims,
and some were just self-willed wanderers, always with itching ears,
but never able to arrive at the truth. They were an unstable scourge
in the monastic world of Benedict. Benedict addresses this by having his monks make a promise of stability in the monastery until
death. They could be assigned under obedience to various ministries and in spearheading monastic foundations from the motherhouse, but they could not just wander at will.

This is powerful for us today. So much of our modern world seems
to be unraveling. Families are unraveling. Morals are unraveling.
Spirituality is unraveling. Polarization and division from within, and
threats from terrorists from without give us all a sense that the stable world we once knew is disintegrating before our very eyes. It is
destabilizing to our very heart and soul, and to our entire culture.

St. Benedict gives us an answer through the stability of a way of life
built squarely on the faith and morality of Jesus Christ, the Church,
and the monastic community. It is more than words, or winning an
argument about politics or moral challenges. It is a way of life built
on the Rock of Jesus Christ. Benedict provides the stability of a
faith-filled community and family life in Christ that can restore our
unraveling culture.

Are you willing to embrace such stability? Benedict offers it to you. Jesus offers it to you. And I offer it to you in their name right now! Will you accept the gift?

Study Questions

1) Do we need a rule of life to give our life some order?

2) Do we really listen to a spiritual father, mother, or elder who is experienced in successful life in Christ and the Church?

3) If we are leaders, are we balanced or abusive?

4) Do we listen to the counsel of many, or do we obstinately hold our opinion as better than others?

5) Do we use Scripture as a primary source for knowing the way of Jesus Christ and as the tool of good works?

6) Do we know the balance between silence and speech?

7) Are we really humble, not only before God, but before others?

8) Are we stable or unstable in our spiritual, moral, and familial foundations in Jesus Christ? Can we make a commitment of stability to remain in our promised way of life until death?

CHAPTER 8: CELTIC MONASTICISM

My ministry trips to Ireland have always been wonderful and spiritually enriching experiences! It began by visiting the Carmelites at Gort Muire, or The Field of Mary Retreat Center, outside of Dublin. There I was introduced to Fr. John Keating, who was a liturgical leader, and Fr. Christopher O'Donnell, the liaison for the Catholic Charismatic Renewal in Ireland. I also visited the Franciscans at Broch House, or The House of Bread, after a large Catholic Charismatic conference at the RDS Arena in Dublin.

I had come to do ministry in charismatic gatherings and Secular Franciscan fraternities after the conference, and I was anxious to get started. I was welcomed with enthusiastic hospitality so typical of both Franciscans and the Irish, ushered into a beautiful modern friary, and fed a wonderful meal before the superior of the house calmly said, "So, John Michael, why are you here?" I was dumbfounded; my contact with the friars had simply forgotten to arrange any ministry for me! So, there I was, having flown across half the American continent and a rather large ocean, with nowhere further to go! But the friars were so great! They gave me a two week stay in any Franciscan house in Ireland, with free travel, room, and board— and any ministry they could arrange. It ended up being a wonderful trip on every level, and sparked my love for Celtic monasticism.

It was on this visit that I got to see first-hand many ruins from the early Celtic monasteries that predate later Roman liturgical influence. I remember the primitive beehive stone huts clustered in groups around a chapel where Celtic monks lived according to the semi-eremitical pattern of Egypt, but in a way adapted to their home terrain and climate. I especially loved Innisfallen in the Lake of Killarney, where the famous Annals of Ireland were written by Celtic monks, just across the shore from Muckross Abbey. While I do regret not being able to visit the famous Skellig Michael due to rough seas, I thoroughly enjoyed the Dingle Peninsula, which embodies so much of what is charming in the Irish spirit.

It was there that I learned *a lot* about the Irish themselves. At every house they welcomed me like Christ, and stayed up well into the wee hours of the morning to swap spiritual stories and songs. They knew the spirituality of the Celts first hand, and not just from books! So a steady stream of stories, poems, and music—lots and lots of music—flowed until 3 or 4 AM! Then, after a couple hours of sleep, we'd rise for Morning Prayer and Mass! I must admit, since I was treated to this wonderful welcome in every house I visited, by the end of two weeks I rather desperately just wanted a full night's sleep!

Years later I would return to Ireland with a country-wide outreach for renewal, with concerts across the island. I used an Augustinian retreat center for my base, and was again treated to wonderful hospitality, but without the all-night spiritual conferences! I must confess that at my older age I was much relieved!

I also visited a splendid place called Glendalough where I got to see an early Celtic monastic ruin founded by St. Kevin and where I heard some wonderful teaching from the local priest, who is an expert in Celtic monasticism. This brought me my clearest understanding yet of this unique monastic tradition.

It is in this Celtic monastic pattern that we see the earliest integration of the patterns of the Desert Fathers of Palestine with the colder climates of Ireland, Scotland, and Wales. The pattern is the same, but with a new Celtic twist—integrated not just into the special climate but the special culture of these places.

The classical threefold monastic catalogue—cenobitical (community), semi-eremitical (colony), and eremitical (solitary)—were integrated in Celtic monasticism into a single monastic organization.

They also developed a threefold integration of celibate men, celibate women, and families in each group. This was done in three concentric circles. The inner circle was for male monks, the second for female monks, or nuns, and the third for families. Each had its own chapel and common areas.

They also integrated another threefold pattern of monastics, clergy, and laity. Keep in mind that these were primarily monastic villages built along the lines of the Celtic tribal village. Large towns and their corresponding dioceses led by bishops, such as were found in continental Europe, simply did not exist in Celtic society. Abbots or abbesses inherited their leadership positions from Celtic royalty as kings and queens, princes and princesses. Consequently, the bishop (who must be male) of the Celtic monastic village might either be the abbot or a monk who was sometimes, strictly speaking, under a female abbess.

The abbot or abbess was responsible for the orderly function and the spiritual fitness of the entire monastic village. The bishop, on the other hand, was responsible for the clergy and the administration of the sacraments within the monastery. Interestingly, while many points, such as the date for Easter or the style of monastic tonsure, were divisive between the Celts and their continental brothers and sisters in Christ, the issue of this integration of monastics, clergy, and laity was not really problematic.

The Celtic monastic model spread across these lands because it successfully baptized the prevailing culture and integrated with it in a way that did not do violence to the aspects that were truly compatible with the Gospel. The Roman model did not do this as easily at first, and was initially unsuccessful. Specifically, the Celtic monastics integrated the structure of the tribal village, the island's troubadour-like bards, and the mystical druids into their monastic model. Celtic monasteries and monks, more so than the Roman model built around larger towns and a desire for logical structure, could baptize and transform small tribal villages and tribal leadership into the local monastery, wandering bards to the itinerant ministry of the wandering monks, and mystics to the mystical experience of the Christian monks. It spread like wildfire!

The physical appearance of Celtic monks was radically different than that of the monks of continental Europe. They had a tonsure which amounted to shaving the head from ears forward and letting hair grow out long in the back. Moreover, they often wore monastic habits that were striped with various colors. The monks of continental Europe, on the other hand, wore the iconic tonsure that included shaving their head on top, leaving hair that was closely cropped in the Roman style. Their monastic attire was more sober as well, usually consisting of dark undyed wool, or wool dyed black as a sign of death to this world.

Celtic spirituality was fiery and vibrant! It included radical calls for repentance and a personal relationship with Jesus Christ that was highly charismatic in the Holy Spirit, yet undeniably Trinitarian. It was fully alive in an appreciation for God's work of outpouring love through creation for all humanity. It also included an emphasis on evangelization of non-Christians and higher education that included copying beautiful manuscripts of ancient sacred and secular classics from Greek and Latin. Celts were simply on fire with a love for God through Jesus Christ, and a zeal for living the Gospel that was unmatched by many or even most in continental Europe. No wonder St. Columbanus would later be so effective in his evangelistic works, spreading renewed Christianity and a fully enlivened monasticism through Europe as far south as northern Italy!

Let's take a look at some great Celtic monastic saints who spread this radical gospel phenomenon so effectively.

St. Palladius

Little is known for certain about the life of St. Palladius, though scholars agree that he was the first bishop of Ireland—before even St. Patrick. In many cases facts and legends about these two great saints have been hopelessly entangled. In other words, some of what has come down to us about Patrick may have actually been about Palladius, and vice versa!

Palladius was born in the late fourth century, probably to a noble family in Gaul (modern France). He seems to have become important in Rome, and was sent to Ireland by Pope Celestine I in 431 as the island's first bishop to minister to the growing number of Christians there. Ireland at that time was still run by clans and warlords, though, so Palladius's reception was chilly.

Nevertheless, he managed to found several churches in Ireland, mainly in the east-central region of Leinster. The tensions with the pagan locals took their toll on Palladius, though, and he eventually returned to Great Britain. While some legends claim he was martyred in Ireland, it's generally agreed that he died in Scotland in the late 450s.

St. Patrick

St. Patrick, the Apostle of Ireland, picked up where Palladius left off. Born around the same time as Palladius in Roman Britain, Patrick entered a Christian family but, like so many other saints we've seen, was not serious about the Faith as a teenager. At 16, though, he was kidnapped by Irish raiders and enslaved for six years across the Irish Sea from his family. According to his own account in his *Confession*, these years were physically grueling but a time of great growth spiritually. It was also during this time that he picked up the Irish language he would later need to minister to the people of the island.

Patrick managed to escape back to his home in Britain, and shortly thereafter he moved to become a priest. As was standard for clergy at the time, he was educated in continental Europe and is said to have visited Marmoutier Abbey and what would later be the Cistercian Lérins Abbey. Even though Patrick didn't found any particular Irish monasteries he was certainly shaped by Western monasticism.

Whereas Palladius left his mark in the east, from which he fled after difficulties with the locals, Patrick's mission territory was primarily in the north and west, where he stayed until his death. The stories and legends told about St. Patrick are too many to mention (and in some cases, like using the shamrock to symbolize the Trinity and driving out the snakes from Ireland, too well-known to mention); Ireland is covered with local tales.

Perhaps the most interesting story for our purposes is that of St. Patrick's weeks-long retreats to a remote island mountain where he would live in solitude in a cave, praying for the Irish people in his time and through the rest of history. It is said that demons in the form of huge ugly birds blanketed the skies and the hillsides, but Patrick would not be deterred, scattering the demons by ringing a beautiful bell, which is held in an Irish reliquary to this day.

It is unclear when exactly Patrick died. Some sources have him living past 100 years old! What is known for sure is that he died in Ireland among the people he had committed himself to in life and in death.

St. Brigit

If St. Patrick is the spiritual father of Ireland, St. Brigit (also Brigid, Bridget, or Bridgit) is the spiritual mother. Miraculous legends about her begin in her infancy (451 or 452), with her refusing to be fed by the vicious druid to whom she had been sold into slavery; instead, a special cow appeared out of nowhere to nourish her.

She took her religious professions as a teenager, becoming the first woman religious in Ireland. But she wasn't alone for long! Her reputation for incredible holiness attracted other women (and men) to the religious life, and by age 30 she was abbess of her own monastery—the famous and beautiful Kildare, or "Church of the Oak."

At Kildare we can see the distinctively Celtic monastic expression begin to take form. Brigit established two communities in separate areas, one for women and the other for men. While the men's community was run by an abbot (and sometimes a bishop-abbot), within the structure of Kildare the abbess was always the superior. As lay people began to come to Kildare to partake of the bright light of holiness that shone from Brigit's communities, a city began to appear.

The fruits of Kildare didn't stop with the town. Brigit's monastery spawned others throughout Ireland. We can say not only that she is the mother of Irish Catholicism, but also that she is the foundress of Irish monasticism.

With dozens of miracles (of various levels of authenticity) attributed to her, Brigit is truly one of the most special women in Church history. She was close friends with St. Patrick, who upon his death was covered in a shroud she made for him. St. Brigit went to her eternal reward on February 1, 525.

St. Columba (Columkille)

Born in 521 of royal lineage in the far northwest of Ireland–County Donegal–St. Columba (also Columkille or Columbkille) was a brilliant and hot-blooded man who left his mark on the Church across Ireland and Scotland. He studied at Clonard Abbey under St. Finnian, where historical sources say there were 3,000 students at any given time.

We should pause to reflect on that number: 3,000! Less than a century earlier St. Palladius had been the very first bishop on this largely pagan island, and now a single monastery was training 3,000 Christian scholars! The Holy Spirit was truly moving through Ireland at that time.

After leaving Clonard, Columba founded several more monasteries across Ireland, from County Derry to Dublin itself. The growth of Christianity and of Christian monasticism in particular was truly incredible!

A rather strange episode in Columba's life demonstrates that even great saints are not beyond petty squabbles–but that God can use those moments when we fall short to still achieve great things. Columba had, without asking, made a copy of a manuscript owned by St. Finnian of Movilla (different from St. Finnian of Clonard) with the intention of keeping the copy. Finnian did not think that Columba should be permitted to keep this copy, and the king ruled with Finnian. The dispute escalated to the point that Columba summoned his clan to rise up against the king, and many men were killed.

The fallout from Columba's actions ultimately led to his leaving Ireland for Scotland. Filled with guilt over the men who died over his personal disputes, he had been given a penance to leave Ireland and to win as many souls for Christ in mission work as were lost in the battle he initiated. The result was again evidence of the working of the Holy Spirit: the founding of the stunning monastery at Iona and the beginning of the conversion of the Picts, or the Celts of Scotland.

Iona is a small tranquil island off the western coast of Scotland. The monastery Columba founded there was one of the most beautiful anywhere in the world, and became the base of operations for the conversion of the people of Scotland. It is one of the few standout Celtic monasteries that I have not had the privilege of visiting—but I hope to someday! After traveling widely in Scotland and bringing the Gospel to thousands upon thousands of people, Columba died on Iona in 597.

Columba's story reminds us that the saints were not perfect men and women; indeed, sometimes their faults were quite serious. But if we come back to God with humility when we fall short, He can use those bad moments to achieve incredible things. For Columba, while the guilt he felt and the penance he was given must have felt like the end of his ministry, due to his faithfulness it turned out to be the beginning of a new and wonderful phase!

St. Columbanus

Columbanus is the quintessential Celtic monastic saint. Born in Ireland in 543, he stayed there for forty years before taking his show—that is, Celtic monasticism!—on the road to continental Europe for the remainder of his life.

He started in Gaul, founding monasteries in the Celtic style in remote wildernesses that became incredibly popular. Columbanus's success began to attract unwanted attention, though, as the local bishops became concerned that this foreign monastic was becoming *too* popular. Disputes erupted over unique aspects of

Celtic Christianity, especially the dating of Easter and the distinct Irish tonsure.

Columbanus's approach to these disputes was consistent: While he was always a zealous defender of orthodoxy, he didn't let himself get pushed around by continental elites on matters, such as the date of Easter and the tonsure, where the essentials of the Faith were not at stake. He would humbly but boldly disagree and hold his ground if he thought it was his duty and right as a faithful Catholic Christian. But he always gave way to legitimate higher authority. He was unfailingly obedient (this is the first and most important point of the monastic rule he created) and so would appeal to the Pope in Rome, whose word would, in his mind, always settle the matter.

There's an important lesson here for us as we try to build new ministries (and strengthen existing ones) in the Church: Diversity in non-essential matters makes our ministries and communities stronger. The form of monastic life Columbanus brought to continental Europe was incredibly appealing to a lot of people for whom the other traditional forms of religious life were not. Don't fight it; embrace it! Provided everyone has a fundamental commitment to the Truth of the Christ and the Catholic faith, diversity in peripheral matters can bring in more people, making our ministries more, well, 'catholic' (or 'universal').

Tensions continued to rise in Gaul, though, especially when Columbanus denounced a Burgundian king for living with his mistress. The saint was literally on a boat back to Ireland when a huge storm forced them back into a French port. Sensing that a "higher power" didn't want them to leave France, the sailors refused to embark again. So Columbanus stayed on the continent.

He ended up founding the beautiful and important monastery of Bobbio near Milan, from which he energetically combatted the Arian heresy, which was still strong in northern Italy (and across

Europe) at that time. St. Columbanus died there in 615 after more than thirty years successfully spreading Celtic monasticism in Gaul and Italy.

St. Aidan

While little is known about the early life of St. Aidan, we can say that he was born in the late sixth century and that his monastic life began at Iona, St. Columba's monastery off the western coast of Scotland. Aidan's calling, however, would be across the island in far northeast England: Northumbria.

Roman Christianity had been brought to this part of Great Britain centuries before, but it was again succumbing to paganism. Aidan, though, brought the vigor of Celtic monasticism to Northumbria, founding a monastery on Lindisfarne, an awesome island of the eastern coast.

I have had the pleasure of visiting Lindisfarne! You can only drive out to the island at low tide, making it impossible to return at high tide, which means you have to spend the night if you miss the tide, regardless of other plans! The solitary hill rising up at one end of the island gives it a mystical aspect. Although some things have changed since the seventh century—the Anglican parish, for instance—it is not difficult to feel the presence of St. Aidan and the first Celtic monks in this holy island today!

The first Irish monk sent to Northumbria left in disgust, having unsuccessfully tried a "fire and brimstone" approach to bringing the Gospel to the people. Aidan, on the other hand, evangelized by building relationships. He became a constant, humble presence in the towns of the region, always walking (rather than riding) from place to place, learning about people's lives and gently introducing the Faith to them. Aidan was also known for his generosity to the vulnerable; he took in numerous orphans, and would often use the contributions of the rich to buy the freedom of slaves, whom he would then educate in the faith, often elevating them to the priesthood.

Sometimes, to be sure, we are called to preach the Gospel uncompromisingly. But sometimes we are called, like Aidan, to be a gentle and humble presence in people's lives. Evangelization can be as simple as making friends!

Aidan's ministry reached a dramatic climax when the pagans of Northumbria, frustrated at his success, tried to burn the royal castle of the Christian king of the region. Aidan's prayers from Lindisfarne are said to have turned the flames on the attackers, who fled, sensing that spiritual forces beyond their understanding were against them. Shortly thereafter in 651, fittingly while on a mission to one of Northumbria's local churches, St. Aidan died.

St. Hilda of Whitby

Perhaps no saint in this book exemplifies the idea of a "monk dynasty" more than St. Hilda, whose monastic ancestors go all the way back to St. Finnian at Clonard in the fifth century (and really even farther back to Ss. Palladius and Patrick). St. Columba studied under St. Finnian and went on to found Iona. Then St. Aidan studied at Iona and went on to found Lindisfarne. Then St. Hilda became a disciple of St. Aidan and went on to found Whitby. It's all in the Celtic monastic family!

Hilda was born into the Northumbrian royal court in 614, and converted as a teenager along with the rest of the court, who followed the king into the Church. While the family grew in faith with many members consecrating themselves to God, wars and political struggles moved them to East Anglia in southeast England.

Hilda intended to leave for Chelles Abbey in Gaul along with her sister, but St. Aidan called her back to found a monastery of her own—Whitby.

Like St Brigit's Kildare, Whitby Abbey was a double monastery in the Celtic pattern with separate communities of men and women. And also like Kildare, the abbess was in charge—even when the abbot of the men's community was a bishop! It was a delicate balance, but Hilda's eminent wisdom and holiness made it work.

Whitby Abbey became so renowned for its holiness and scholarship that the king of Northumbria selected it as the location for the Synod of Whitby, the first gathering of its kind in Britain. The topic to be discussed was the differences between the Celtic and Roman Churches, especially the date of Easter and the Irish tonsure. While Hilda favored the Celtic position, the king ultimately sided with the Roman position on both issues, establishing them as the norm. While some Celtic officials retired to Iona or all the way back to Ireland in response, Hilda remained in what is now Britain until her death in 680.

The Synod of Whitby marked the beginning of the end of Celtic monasticism, which became limited to Ireland and Scotland. There were good reasons for adopting the Roman calendar and tonsure, but we also can't help but be a little sad to see this astonishing and beautiful era in Christian monastic history fade away. Today, there are many who seek to resurrect the best of the Celtic monastic tradition in a way that is appropriate for the tradition in which they find themselves.

St. Brendan

Before we move on, though, let's briefly look at one more Celtic saint who has a special claim to fame. St. Brendan was born in 484 in the southwestern Irish province of Munster. He went on, like so many others (including St. Columba) to study under St. Finnian at Clonard. After leaving Clonard, Brendan founded several monasteries throughout the south and west of Ireland, and several more on islands around Ireland that he visited by sea.

It is Brendan's seafaring ways that became legendary, as later stories tell of an incredible seven-year journey to a lush paradise way out in the ocean west of Ireland. For centuries afterward maps contained references to "St. Brendan's Island," but the place was never found. Some believe that St. Brendan made it all the way to North America, beating the Norse by 500 years and Columbus by a millennium! It's impossible to say what really happened, but the Irish are happy to claim they got here first!

Whether it was after a harrowing journey to the New World, or just a tour around Ireland, Brendan ended up visiting Columba's monastery at Iona for a few years, apparently meeting Columba himself. He then returned to Ireland to found the last of his many monasteries, this one at Annaghdown, where he died around the year 577 at older than 90 years. He left behind not only the legendary tale of his voyages, but place names around western Ireland and even Britain that testify to his missionary zeal.

Celtic Expansion

Today the Celtic monastic model has so much to teach us! It reminds us to adapt Christianity to local customs in a way that doesn't compromise the essence of the faith, but in fact spreads it ever more powerfully! It is in the diversity of expressions of Catholicism that its universality is made clear. The so-called New Monasticism that is spreading in North America and Europe can find wonderful precedence in Celtic monasticism regarding the integration of spiritualities and states of life. But the Celtic success should never be used as an excuse for extreme and careless integrations. To use a musical example: We should not be aiming for the artificial integrity produced by a synthesizer, which makes one sound appear to be something it is not through the distortion of another. This is often heard in the "close, but not quite" sounds of strings and orchestras that are so common today. Rather, proper spiritual integration is more like a rope or cord, which retains the integrity of each strand, winding them together such that it makes the whole stronger than any individual part. When the sound of the synthesizer is unique to that media, and clearly a synthetic sound nothing else can produce, then it is great! When it tries to be something it is not through the distortion and forced combination of other legitimate sounds, it is not. It's just a cheap imitation. Celtic monasticism did this properly in a healthy integration that revolutionized pagan Celtic culture through a full baptism in Christ. It retained the authentic beauty of Celtic culture, and completed it through the catholicity that only Jesus Christ can bring!

Study Questions

1)   How does the integrated pattern of a monasticism of monks, nuns, and families inspire us today?

2)   What is the difference between an integration that retains the integrity of each state of life, and a synthesis that confuses and distorts them by making them appear to be something they are not?

3)   In Whitby Hilda was the abbess of a double abbey of monks and nuns where one of the monks was the local bishop. How does the delicate balance of a lay abbess and bishop in the same double monastery speak to us

today? How do we balance male and female, lay and clerical leadership in monasteries and parishes?

4) Celtic monasticism was adapted to Celtic culture, and was wildly successful. How do we adapt ancient monastic and Catholic patterns to our specific culture today? What is too much, and what is too little? Is our evangelization really effective in our culture today?

5) The Synod of Whitby in 663-664 effectively began the end of the Celtic Rite in the Catholic Church in the West. How do we accept the valid decisions of the synods and ecumenical councils of the Church that might develop, change, or terminate traditions we have held dear for decades, or even centuries?

CHAPTER 9: THE REFORMERS: BRINGING THE ANCIENT FAITH INTO THE NOW

Do you ever feel like your life needs to be reformed—like somehow you've allowed yourself to slide into a lifestyle different from what God wants for you? Guess what? Jesus has an answer!

Scripture speaks of repentance and reform. "From that time on, Jesus began to preach and say, 'Repent, for the kingdom of heaven is at hand.'"(Mt. 4:17) The Greek for "repent" is μετανοέω (*meta-noeo*), which means to change with your thoughts. It comes from μετά (*meta*), which means "with," and νοέω (*noeo*), which means "mind." Remember, we have the "mind of Christ" (1 Cor. 2:16) and are called to have a spiritual "renewal of the mind." (Rom. 12:2)

But the original New American Bible translated Matthew 4:17 not as "repent" but as "reform your lives." While not as true to the original Greek, I liked it! Reform literally means to be "formed again." We often allow ourselves to fall into a deformed version of what God wants for us, and therefore we need reform.

But this also applies to the Church, and spiritual movements, ministries, and communities within the Church. Do you ever feel like the Christianity of our time has somehow veered from the original purity of the Church in the time of Christ and the apostles? The same has been true of almost every era in the Church, and reform is necessary.

Sometimes we only think of the Protestant Reformation when we think about reform. But that is incorrect, or at least incomplete. There have been many reforms throughout the history of the Church.

There is a pattern of founding, deforming, and reforming that repeats in the Church in the movements, ministries, and communities raised up by the Spirit throughout history. In monasticism we can see this regularly repeating about every 100-200 years. Nowadays, because of the immediacy of communication via technology, we see it happening much more quickly.

In the 10th and 11th centuries we see three primary reformers of the Benedictine tradition, although one is not strictly Benedictine: St. Romuald, St Bruno, and St. Bernard of Clairvaux. The first two brought the semi eremitical life from Egypt and early European monasticism into the West, and the third reformed the cenobitical expression.

A handy way to remember these reforms is the "three C's": Camaldolese, Carthusian, and Cistercian. Though there were other similar communities, it is the three C's that endured through history, and are still with us today.

Western monasticism had been planted firmly by pioneers like St. Benedict, and it prospered! It spread due to the purity of its vision for the religious life. Monastic empires like Cluny spread across Europe, and they blessed both the Church and the world with countless ministries. But prosperity brought financial supporters who donated to help the life and work of the monks. Soon the monasteries grew rich and powerful. With that power came corruption. And with corruption came laxity, worldliness, and the need to reform according to the patterns that made them successful in the first place. Sound familiar? It should. It happens throughout history, and it is still happening today.

While each of these reforms brought unique gifts to the Church, they all attempted to return to the early Egyptian pattern of cenobitical, semi-eremitical, and reclusive life, with outreach into mission. Camaldolese spirituality, for instance, focused specifically on the "threefold good," while the other two did so at least by implication. The strictly contemplative Carthusians gave us incredible written spiritual masterpieces, either named or authored anonymously. And the Cistercians revolutionized agriculture through their Grange system and gave us holy men and women such as St. Bernard of Clairvaux, who was arguably the most influential man in Europe in his time. They also were most helpful to St. Dominic Guzman in the 13th century in the founding of his contemplative and apostolic missions in the Order of Preachers—known as the Dominicans.

Study Questions

1) Do we need periodic personal and communal reform? How?

2) What does repentance mean to you?

3) How does founding, deforming, and reforming apply to our life and time? Is it personal for you? Does it have communal dimensions in your family, community, ministry, parish, or place of work?

4) What are the three C's, and how well do we remember the lessons of the past in living in today's Church and world?

St. Romuald

By all appearances, Romuald led a normal life for a son of a noble family in the northeast Italian city of Ravenna. He was born in luxury in 951 and lived a worldly life. But God had greater things in store for Romuald than just enjoying earthly pleasures.

As a young adult Romuald served as a second to his father in a duel in which his father killed a family member. The episode, while not entirely uncommon in tenth-century Ravenna, devastated Romuald, and he went off to the Benedictine Basilica of Sant'Apollinaire in Classe to do 40 days of penance for his father's sin. He felt drawn to the lifestyle of the Benedictine monks and decided to abandon his profligate life in favor of the monastic life.

He finished his novitiate, but soon became discouraged by the laxity of the cenobitical life in his community. He discerned a call to the solitude he learned about in the sayings and lives of the early monastic fathers and mothers and retired to a primitive hermitage with a rustic lay hermit named Marinus.

A funny story is told about this pair: Romuald memorized the Psalter under the direction of Marinus, who would box Romuald's ear every time he made a mistake. After almost going deaf from being boxed repeatedly on one side, he humbly asked Marinus to strike the other ear for a while! Though this would never fly in today's educational environment, and I would not recommend it for any parent or religious teacher, it demonstrates Romuald's determination to stick with his task despite hardships.

In those days hermits and holy men and women often became famous. This was true especially when they were from the upper class of society. The conversion and holy life of someone of secular power not only attracted crowds and eventually disciples, but also got the attention of bishops and secular rulers in Christian Europe.

Many of these secular leaders were devoted sons and daughters of the Church, and desired to spread the Gospel to lands and peoples who had yet to hear the good news of Jesus Christ. Of course, they sometimes had ulterior motives, such as expanding their own secular power and the financial gain that such expansion promised.

As for Romuald, he attracted the attention of the young Holy Roman Emperor Otto III, who had been crowned King of Germany at age three and had marched into Italy at age 16. At the ripe old age of 19, Otto made a pilgrimage to visit Romuald, seeking penance for having executed a political opponent whose safety he had previously assured. The emperor prevailed on Romuald to return to where his monastic life began—Sant'Apollinaire—as abbot to reform the monastery.

He accepted this leadership role, but the monks began to realize that they got more than a famous hermit as their new abbot; they got a serious reformer—and they didn't want to be reformed! So the good monks did what all good monks did in those days when they got an abbot they couldn't live with: They tried to poison him! Now remember, this also happened in Gregory the Great's Life of St. Benedict, so this story has a profound symbolic significance. And like St. Benedict, instead of fighting the monks, Romuald dramatically resigned by throwing the abbatial staff down before the emperor and stating loudly that he would never accept it again. This was a promise he maintained throughout his life. He withdrew once more into the beloved solitude of the hermitage.

But Romuald wasn't totally isolated. He moved to a hermitage connected with a monastery that sought his help, so that he could be a reforming influence through his example and teaching. This became a pattern: He would establish an abbot who would embody his reform, stay for a while, and move on to another monastery.

Some say he reformed or founded almost 100 monasteries during his long life!

In the beginning the Camaldolese were simply called "Romualdians" after their founder. (I know, it sounds like Romulans from Star Trek!) They were eventually called "Camaldolese" after Camaldoli, that monastery which became the most famous of those who followed the Romualdian reform. There is even some scholarly doubt as to whether or not Romuald even visited Camaldoli personally during his lifetime! But they certainly embodied Romuald's charism beautifully. Interestingly, it was at Camaldoli that St. Francis of Assisi and Cardinal Hugolino (later Pope Gregory IX) met to discuss the multitudes of lay people and diocesan clergy who were associating with the Franciscan movement, laying out the first Rule of the Third Order of Penitents, called the Secular Franciscan Order after Vatican II.

Romuald spent roughly the last three decades of his life criss-crossing Italy founding and reforming numerous monasteries. He followed a pattern: He would show up at a monastery and live as a reclusive hermit, leading by example. Without taking on formal leadership he would attract new followers and reform older monks. Once he felt the reform had really taken hold, he would appoint a new abbot and move on to a new challenge. As he had prophesied many years before, Romuald died alone in his cell in 1027.

Romuald reformed monasteries by reestablishing the ancient pattern of cenobites, semi-eremites, and recluses. But he added another dimension that has often been overlooked, but that is being rediscovered today. That dimension is mission! Many forget that the first missionary martyrs in Poland were Camaldolese monks! With the support of the Emperor, Romuald sent out his first five missionary brothers, all of whom were martyred in Poland. Their end was brutal, but bore much fruit as word got out about the barbaric way in which they were killed. This provides ample inspiration for us today as we face increasing persecution in the secular humanist West, not to mention at the hands of Muslim extremists in the Middle East.

Romuald's success gave birth to his "Threefold Good," which consisted of the cenobium, the hermitage, and the mission (or community, solitude, and ministry). This produced many missionaries in the West who contributed to sacred and secular arts on many levels. One example is the monk, Guido of Arezzo (c. 992-1050), who formed the foundation for modern musical notation. And Gratian (d. 1160) used a compilation of over 4,000 patristic, conciliar, and papal texts in his *Decretum* in such a way that avoided rigid legalism; he is now called "the father of canon law." These are only two out of dozens of examples. Who would think this would come forth from an order dedicated to solitude and contemplative prayer?

Furthermore, it was the Camaldolese who offered a place of refuge to the Capuchin Franciscans who were being persecuted by their own brothers for wanting to return to the contemplative dimension of their own Rule. Actually it was the Observant Order of Friars Minor (Franciscan) Bernadine Reformers, also trying to re-establish the semi eremitical life, who sought to shut them down because they were trying to achieve a competing reform! The Camaldolese inadvertently contributed to the distinctly long pointed hermit hoods, or capuches, from which the Capuchins got their name!

But for me, as much as I like the Camaldolese model, Romuald's Brief Rule for Hermits remains something that sings in my soul. I have set it to music and recorded it, but have yet to include it on an album of songs. Yet, in its quaint brevity the entire life of the hermit sings. Here is the rule:

> Sit in your cell as in paradise. Put the whole world
> behind you and forget it. Watch your thoughts like a

good fisherman watching for fish. The path you must follow is in the Psalms – never leave it.

Question: How do you provide for times and places of undistracted solitude and silence?

If you have just come to the monastery, and in spite of your good will you cannot accomplish what you want, take every opportunity you can to sing the Psalms in your heart and to understand them with your mind.

Question: Do you pray the Psalms? Do you pray the Liturgy of the Hours? How does Scripture meditation, or Lectio Divina, play into your prayer time?

And if your mind wanders as you read, do not give up; hurry back and apply your mind to the words once more.

Question: How do you deal with distractions during prayer? Do you get anxious and upset by them, or calmly bring your mind back to God?

Realize above all that you are in God's presence, and stand there with the attitude of one who stands before the emperor.

Question: Do you approach prayer as a sacred time, or is it so casual that you easily forget it or do it "catch as catch can?"

Empty yourself completely and sit waiting, content with the grace of God, like the chick who tastes nothing and eats nothing but what his mother brings him.

Question: During prayer do you allow your old self to die with Christ and rise up a completely new creation in Him? This is, after all, the main point of all Christian prayer from the personal perspective.

Personal Experience

But, it's not enough to simply read about monasteries; you must visit them if at all possible. It is in their everyday life that you see biographies and rules lived out by real people. Fortunately, I've been able to visit the Camaldolese at Big Sur, California, here in the United States on several occasions. Early on I also asked to visit the Primitive Reform branch of Camaldolese Hermits in Steubenville, Ohio, but received a very sweet letter written out in an old man's shaky hand discouraging me from visiting. I remember with some humor that he said they really didn't like music there. I was not offended; in fact their faithfulness warmed my heart!

The Camaldolese at Big Sur were very welcoming. On my initial visit I remember visiting with the prior at the time, Prior Bruno. I found it interesting that he had chosen, or had been given, the name of the founder of the Carthusians!

The biggest single thing I remember from that visit was Prior Bruno's taking many hours to discuss the Camaldolese tradition of the semi-eremitical life with me. We talked about history, hermits, and holy monks—Camaldolese, Desert Fathers, Benedictines, and Franciscans. It was an engaging in depth dialogue about the entire tradition, and my place in it. He invited me to New Camaldoli. I ended up choosing another semi-eremitical path for my community, but the Camaldolese charism has remained a powerful inspiration for me as founder of a new semi-eremitical community in our own time. I remain a bit of a "closet Camaldolese" in my heart!

Over the years I remember him saying that many of the young inquirers to the Hermitage come and want to spend all their time at prayer in solitude. But he said with some humor that they had to learn first how to live in community with each other, and that he needed them to work in the bakery for a living! This is something I would learn and often remember in a very personal way as Founder and General Minister of the Brothers and Sisters of Charity at the Little Portion Hermitage. But of all the things he shared I really remember one thing most. Before leaving my guest cell after our final talk, he turned and rather whimsically said, "Remember, only characters come here!" In other words, it is not a lifestyle for many, but should inspire us all!

I spent many hours during that first visit walking in the mountains above the Holy Hermitage. The place is stunning! It sits on a steep hill, almost a cliff, about 1500 feet above the Pacific Ocean, with even taller mountains above it. In the mornings I watched the fog burn away from the ocean below, seemingly on a majestic precipice above the fray of ordinary secular life.

The hermitages are arranged in a typical fashion, scattered around a common chapel, refectory, and work buildings. The guest house is separate from the monk's hermitages, but visitors are made most welcome, sharing all prayer services and even some meals. All guests can ask for spiritual direction while there.

The Divine Office and Mass are above the average experience by Western monastic standards. The simple chanted office was especially lovely, and unlike anything found in parish churches or most active religious houses. It positively impacted what chant tones I would later choose for our Little Portion services.

On one of my walks I encountered a lay monk who lived as a recluse in the hill above the Hermitage. He prayed, worked, and ate in reclusion, only coming to the Hermitage once a week for Sunday Eucharist, and the weekly community meeting and meal. Though only a lay monk, no less than Bishop Fulton Sheen used to receive spiritual counsel from him! His story illustrated in actual life, rather than just in theory, that the Camaldolese are the only surviving 11th century reform that included the ancient Desert Father practice of reclusion in addition to semi-eremitism and cenobitism. Romuald himself often retired into strict reclusion, at one point for seven straight years, from which he reformed numerous monasteries by his holy example.

Lastly, my old friend Cyprian Consiglio, who is now the Prior of New Camaldoli, demonstrates the third aspect of Camaldolese charism: Mission. Prior Cyprian is not only a well-studied and gifted writer of books, but an accomplished musician of contemporary music, world music, and sacred chant; he frequently toured parishes on the West Coast teaching Christian prayer and meditation using music. He carries on the Camaldolese musical and mission tradition.

Study Questions

1) How does the threefold good of community, hermitage, and mission relate to your life in Christ today?

2) Do you need times of "reclusion?" How does this affect your family, community, or work?

3) Do you pray the Psalter? Have you tried praying the Liturgy of the Hours?

4) How do you use leadership responsibility in your life? Are you willing to step aside and let others take the reins at times?

5) Are you willing to give your life in "martyrdom" for Christ? How do you do that already in your daily life in the modern world?

Carthusians

I have also had the distinct pleasure of visiting the Carthusians at St. Hugh's Charterhouse at Parkminster in Sussex, England. Carthusians normally receive only hermits or prospective members, but I qualified due to my semi-eremitical life. It was an honor!

It was very different than my Camaldolese experience, but no less rewarding! St. Hugh's is an ancient monastery impacted by the Protestant reformers' persecution of Carthusians. The memory of the gruesome martyrdom of their Carthusian brothers still lingers large in their corporate memory, and frescos of the martyrdoms on the refectory ceiling shock us into remembering our terrible past, hopefully so we never repeat it.

Like a medieval pilgrim I came through the walls to the big wooden doors at the entrance and rang the bell. It was a real bell, complete with a rope pull by the doors! Then, I waited. I seem to recall that I waited for some time. Soon the doors opened, and an aging brother welcomed me. He was clear that my guitar, which had accompanied me to monasteries around the world, would not be allowed in. (The prior would later shake his head at this, after asking me to sing some of my songs into his tape recorder, which I did *a cappella*.)

I was ushered into a large guesthouse—the stately mansion of the man who had donated the land long ago. I was alone in this huge, cavernous place! (I must admit praying extra hard through one stormy night when a strong wind blew the attic shutters open and shut with loud bangs that reverberated through the empty mansion!) I made my way to Evening Prayers and Vigils with no light, feeling my way along in the dark. I participated as the lone inhabitant from a balcony at the back of the monastic church. It was moving, but removed.

The next day I met with Prior Bernard, who had come to the Carthusians from the Cistercians at Mellerary Abbey in Ireland, where he had been the Novice Master, or the person in charge of new members. But he felt called to greater solitude, which he found with the Carthusians.

Prior Bernard was a kindly man who asked me all about my integrated life of hermitage, community, and ministry. He explained the Carthusian life, describing the different states of life in the monastery: choir monks who are clerical hermits in the semi-eremitical life, lay brothers who live the cenobitical ideal in community, manual laborers, or conversi, who wear the habit but do not take vows, and domestics who neither wear the habit nor take vows, but help with the work of the community. During my time there I also saw lay workers from outside the monastery helping with the farm.

Prior Bernard showed me around the Charterhouse, complete with a five acre cloister, an impressive library, the main church, the cenobium for the lay brothers and conversi, the chapter room, and the refectory where they all share a weekly common meal. He also let me sample their famous Chartreuse liquor, to be consumed artfully and not for inebriation, and explained that it is a secret recipe only known to the Prior General for the entire Order.

The hermitages themselves are roomy two-story cottages connected to the large cloister by an enclosed walkway with a garden in between. The hermitage has four rooms, two downstairs for cottage industry and repairs, the hermit's main cell with two alcoves for a bed and a *prie dieu*, a desk, and a wood-burning stove. There is also the Ave Maria, which used to serve as the monk's kitchen, but is now empty except for a simple Marian statute. This developed since some more austere monks suffered from malnutrition due to too little food, and now have meals delivered to each cell from a central kitchen.

Keep in mind that the hermit only leaves the hermitage three times a day for Vigils at midnight, Lauds (Morning Prayer and Mass), and Vespers (Evening Prayer). They also eat one common meal together weekly, meet in chapter to discuss and conduct community business, and take a recreational walk through the countryside around the Charterhouse. This last practice keeps them connected with each other and their neighbors.

Prior Bernard invited me to sit next to him in choir to chant the Office with the monks and lay brothers, who now pray together instead of in separate parts of the chapel. We prayed three-to-a-book from huge sheepskin Latin psalters with wonderful illuminated pages. When the older monk sitting next to me asked why I wasn't singing, I responded that I didn't know Latin. I'll never forget his gruff response: "That doesn't matter. Sing!" So I sang, and picked up some Latin along the way! It taught me to sing, not by emotions or intellect alone but in order to glorify God through praise and thanksgiving. It's a lesson I still carry with me today.

The prior also shared a story about how, as a new novice, he was asked to read in Latin. Now, Bernard had been an accomplished medical doctor before his monastic life, and a well-studied priest and leader at the Cistercian Abbey of Mellerary in Ireland. He knew Latin perfectly, but his Novice Master wanted to humble him. So while doing one of the readings during the Office, he stopped him in the middle, corrected him publicly and calmly for sloppy Latin, and sent him to the lowest place in the rank of the community in choir. But here's the lesson: instead of being angry, Bernard was grateful to have been humbled. He assured me that often "humility only comes through humiliation." This is very counter-cultural, and can only be practiced by those seeking a higher call in Christ; otherwise it breeds anger and resentment. Few could muster such faith and humility today.

Prior Bernard followed tradition by showing me the least desirable hermit's cell in order to test whether that would deter me from my call. There were cobwebs everywhere; the place looked like rats were the primary inhabitants! He really wanted me to join them, and truly of all the monasteries I have visited the Carthusians are the ones who impressed me the most. But Prior Bernard admitted that many would-be Carthusians went on to found communities, and he seemed to discern that this would be my call as well. I'll never forget the last private Mass we celebrated in his Prior's Chapel, where we both wept holy tears. We parted as dear spiritual friends who would not see one another again until we meet in heaven. Prior Bernard is now waiting for me there!

The Carthusians are the strictest order in the Catholic Church. They are among the 11th century monastic reformers, but claim the motto: Never reformed, never deformed! It is a very organized Western version of the semi-eremitical monastic ideal of the Desert Fathers. It conserved an ancient tradition that had been rediscovered in the West while adapting it to the more organized and logical modes of thinking and living in the West.

One last point: The Carthusians are most zealous in maintaining a high degree of saintliness that includes spending almost no energy or funds on the process of canonizing their saints. A few are known to us, but most are not. We can see this humility in their death rituals. Upon death a Carthusian monk receives a fitting funeral Mass, but is then placed into a grave behind the monastery with no casket. He is laid to rest protected only by the habit, or monastic garb, he wore in life, with his cowl, or monastic hood, simply drawn over his face. The grave is marked with no name, and just a simple phrase in Latin that says, in effect: "He did alright!" Pray that we can all similarly "do alright" in the sight of God when we finally go to meet Him!

The Carthusians integrated three, and then four, ways of being a part of the community: the choir monk who was a priest and a hermit who professed solemn vows, the lay brother who lived in the cenobium in simple vows, the conversi who wore the habit like the lay brother but without vows, and the domestic who wore secular clothes and shared in the life of the lay and conversi brothers without vows. The genius of this was that it maintained a most strict semi-eremitical way of life, but in a way that made participation in the community available to many men from many backgrounds.

St. Bruno

Like St. Romuald, St. Bruno was born into a prominent noble family. Unlike Romuald, however, Bruno was German and is said to have been a studious boy. He was born in Cologne in 1030 and completed his education at the university in Reims, France, where from 1057 to 1075 he held important administrative and academic posts.

Bruno's life took a turn in 1075 when he was appointed chancellor of the Diocese of Reims. Shortly thereafter the bishop died and was replaced by what we would today call a "political appointee" named Manasses. The new bishop was erratic and violent, and Bruno put himself at risk to seek his removal from the post. After Manasses's final removal in 1080, Bruno was the natural choice to take over the diocese, but he refused the office, desiring to renounce all worldly goods (including those of Church governance) and live the eremitical life.

Bruno conceived the Carthusian ideal—a version of the Desert Fathers more clerical and organized than the originals, and more suited to the culture of Western Europe—during a life-changing encounter with a few friends during a spiritual retreat. During that time they promised that they would all come together at a later date to pursue a life of contemplative solitude. Bruno followed that call with his whole heart and soul. Unfortunately, one brother did not, but he did go on to be ordained as a priest and even a bishop. Keep in mind, though, that through most of Church history monastic life was considered a higher charismatic calling than secular, or diocesan ordination. This is no longer the case strictly speaking, but should not be forgotten as we face a monastic decline in the West. While maintaining friendship with him and honoring his ordination, Bruno never ceased praying for his conversion to honor the original commitment he had made to God, and even wrote him towards the end of his life to gently call him home to that call through repentance.

After declining the job in Reims, Bruno and his comrades sought support from the Bishop of Grenoble in the mountains of southeastern France for their new community. The bishop, who would later be known as St. Hugh, was enthusiastic about Bruno's contemplative community. He gave them land high in the French Alps where they could study and pray in rudimentary cabins.

Imagine not only living in solitude, but living in solitude in uninsulated wooden shacks among some of the tallest, most rugged, and most unpredictable mountain peaks in the world! Needless to say, Bruno's community of hermitages was faced with serious struggles and trials in those early years—including an avalanche that prompted a relocation into the valley. What came next for the Carthusians and Bruno himself, though, is a reminder of how trust in God's plan is rewarded, even when it seems like nature itself is fighting us.

This new location became the site of the now-famous Grande Chartreuse, or Grand Charterhouse. The original Charterhouse is made up of hermit cells around a covered cloister walkway to protect them from the deep Alpine snows. This pattern is now repeated wherever there are Charterhouses, regardless of snow accumulation! The Charterhouses also include a cenobitical monastic dormitory for lay brothers, conversi, and domestics, attached to the common church, chapter room, refectory, and work buildings. They form a veritable village of prayer—a powerhouse of purity to combat the evils of this world through the Spirit-filled enlightenment of the monks who quietly contemplate Jesus and Mary. They are the unseen jewels of our Church and our world.

A Reform, But Not Benedictine

Ironically, while Benedictinism was the predominant form of monastic life in the West, the Carthusians are not, strictly speaking, Benedictine. Though clearly inspired by ancient monasticism and the eremitism spoken of by the Rule of Benedict, rather than professing the Rule of Benedict they eventually professed the Constitutions of Guigo, a prior who succeeded St. Bruno. The Carthusians were bold enough to try something new! They simply lived the semi-eremitical life according to the teaching of St. Bruno. We know of nothing in his writings that would include a rule-like description of their way of life. That was left to later generations. It eventually fell to Guigo to draft the first formal constitutions for the Carthusians. Bruno dared to try something ancient, yet new in his own day, and left us something that inspired us to this day!

This says much to us from all states of life today! We must also be willing to consider reforms of the older expressions of community by using new forms of community life. It neither disregards the ancient, not is enslaved to it. Bruno teaches us this lesson from 1000 years ago!

Self-Support

The monks have tried several means of self-support throughout the centuries, adapting to the needs of the time and the environment in which they find themselves. Through the centuries this has gone from forestry, to ore smithies, to the modern Chartreuse Liquor. (The yellow-green color chartreuse is in fact named for the unique hue of the herbal liqueur!) This teaches us that what powers the engine of their charism is not external work, but an interior and solitary contemplative life in Christ and the Church.

Bruno and Church Authority

In 1088 Bruno's former student, Eudes of Châtillon, became Pope Urban II. With political and ecclesiastical trouble on all sides, Urban summoned his friend Bruno to the Papal court as an advisor. Bruno reluctantly obeyed, leaving behind his brothers at Grand Chartreuse.

Bruno's proximity to the Holy Father—he lived in the same building and had Urban's complete trust—would have made him one of the most influential men in the world. And yet he was very unhappy. During his tenure in Rome, for the second time he was offered a prestigious post in the hierarchy, this time as Archbishop of Reggio Calabria. And for a second time he refused.

Bruno wanted nothing more than to return to his home in southern France, but Urban wanted to keep him close should he need Bruno's advice and support. The pope therefore permitted him to found a community in nearby Calabria in southern Italy, where he stayed until his death in 1101.

Lessons

As I saw at the Carthusian monastery in England, St. Bruno managed to create an organizational structure that permitted those with different vocations to live out those callings in an integrated community without jeopardizing or compromising the integrity of the strict semi-eremitical life. In fact this arrangement protects it! The brilliance of this arrangement is in setting up these diverse vocations in a way that respects their individuality, while ordering them to the good of the monastic community as a whole.

Perhaps what strikes me most about Bruno is neither his love for solitude nor his organizational genius. Rather, it is his obedience to stay in Calabria at the Pope's command to the point of never seeing his beloved brothers at the Grande Chartreuse again in his life! His letters give a clear indication of just how much he loved them, and longed for the Alpine solitude of his original house at the Grande Chartreuse. But he remained obedient, staying in a nice enough but nonetheless very different hillside in Calabria.

From there the Carthusian Order would grow into a powerhouse of solitary semi-eremitical monasticism that spread throughout the Western Church. This, in turn, gave birth to a veritable library of spiritual masterpieces written by men whose names we know, such as Hugh of St. Victor and Denis the Carthusian, and those whose names are known only to God, written by the Spirit in heaven. "They Speak By Silences" has become one such classic work on prayer written by an anonymous Carthusian author.

Study Questions

    1)   Do you ever feel like you need to seek out solitude after times of intense professional duties?

2) Do you see a need for order and organization in a movement raised up by the Holy Spirit? Does that help or hinder the work of the Spirit? Does this take balance?

3) How well do you adapt to the needs and signs of the times in supporting a faith community or spiritual movement? What are the organizational and ministerial dimensions to this adaptation? Does this affect the truth of the charism and call in Christ?

4) How do you relate to friends who began a spiritual journey or commitment with you, but did not fulfill their part?

5) How do you respond in obedience to the Church? Are you willing to set aside your personal preferences or opinions for the greater good of the Church?

St. Bernard of Clairvaux and the Cistercians

I remember fondly my first visit to Our Lady of Gethsemani, the abbey of the Order of Cistercians of the Strict Observance where Thomas Merton lived as America's most published and famous monk. I arrived for the first time in the midst of a gentle winter snow. How well I remember the sound of monastic chant wafting upwards in the spartan monastery church. Somehow I always hear Western chant rising gently from snowy and quiet winter woods to this day. I remember the sound of monks' habits as they walked in and out of the Office. I remember the smell of incense in that holy church from a monastery that has faithfully stood the test of time since the early days of Catholicism in eastern North America. I remember my walks in the woods past Merton's hermitage, and to the top of the Kentucky knolls where the monks enshrined the old spires taken from the church steeple after Vatican II in order to reclaim the simplicity of the early Bernardine Cistercians. Since then I have had the pleasure to visit many Cistercian monasteries, but it is this first visit that stays in my heart and soul to this day. Yes, I love the Cistercian charism; it is a spiritual treasure I hold dear.

Founding

The first Cistercians were Cluniac monks from Molesme who sought a more authentic life according to the Rule of St. Benedict. Molesme itself was a reform community attempting the same, but finding it difficult to break free of the powerful patterns of Cluny. Robert was the abbot of Molesme and was part of the first group of monks who went to Cîteaux, or the "place by the spring," to pioneer a whole new monastic life. The monks of Molesme protested, eventually petitioning the pope to order Robert back to be their abbot. Robert obeyed, and left Stephen Harding in charge at Cîteaux.

The life of the first monks at Cîteaux was terribly hard, as monastic beginnings tend to be. They were dirt poor, lived in crudely constructed huts, drained and cleared by hand the swampland they had been "donated," and literally starved through fasting and simple fare. But they prayed hard too. Boy, did they pray! And God soon responded by sending Bernard and his companions, who arrived unannounced but immediately set to making the place a thriving new monastery. From there it boomed into the single most powerful reform of the 11th century!

Bernard and Family Arrive

St. Bernard of Clairvaux was born in 1090 as a member of the nobility of Burgundy, in central France. Like St. Bruno and St. Romuald before him, Bernard eagerly gave up the worldly advantages of his station to pursue monastic life.

From an early age Bernard excelled in his studies and, the stories say, in virtue. At the age of 22, three years after his mother had died, the young Bernard received in prayer a specific calling to the Cistercian monks at Cîteaux. Bernard's witness was so compelling that thirty other young Burgundian noblemen showed up with him at Cîteaux, and ultimately his five brothers and father joined him as well. Cîteaux, the Cistercians, and all of the Western Church would never be the same.

What strikes me here is that the first Cistercians under Stephen Harding and companions were very poor and obscure. Some would say that they were on the verge of failure. It is only with the arrival of Bernard with his few dozen family members, friends, and companions that the tide turned. Suddenly, almost overnight, they became a large community with many new, young, and bright recruits. Like attracts like. Success attracts successful people. So, the Cistercians began to grow at a phenomenal rate. They spread across Europe, reforming monasticism and the Western Catholic Church.

The same is true with us. Sometimes we must just hang on during the founding stage of a community or ministry. If we are faithful, God will often send a "St. Bernard" into our life to take our vision to the next level. It happens in businesses. It happens in monasteries and Church movements. And it happens in parishes and dioceses. Pray that we might be wise enough to let these modern St. Bernards work freely—once they are properly formed in our own spirituality or charism—and humble enough to let these special people adjust our plans and visions.

Simplicity and Reform

The Cistercians under Bernard embraced a simplicity that pervaded their lifestyle, liturgy, and architecture. Their architecture can be studied in both the ruins and extant houses. Their lifestyle is spelled out in famous Cistercian writings, and in the surviving records of their chapters, or meetings of the abbots of all the monasteries.

St. Bernard simplified their liturgy radically. In a way almost presaging the simple living movement of later Anabaptist tradition, they allowed for no ornamentation in their churches, and only the plainest of monastic chant. Their churches were whitewashed, with only a cross without the body of Jesus! What is interesting is that this simply did not last past the life of St. Bernard. The monks meekly, but surely replaced the extreme simplicity with one that was more livable. They put the corpus, or body of Jesus, back on the cross to remind the monks of the what Jesus did for each one of them personally and communally, allowed for some simply statuary, and so on, while being careful to maintain the simplicity they all loved. This cautions us against extremes, and teaches us that more moderate movements toward the Christian ideal tend to work better, even in a monastic expression.

Granges

One of the most distinct aspects of Cistercian expansion is their use of the Grange system. In fact, the Cistercians revolutionized rural life all across Europe, sometimes to the chagrin of those who hung on to past patterns. Today we still see their vestiges in rural America, but in medieval Europe they were on the cutting edge of creativity!

Cistercians tried to return to a primitive application of the Rule of St. Benedict through their unifying document, the Charter of Charity. The defining feature was a return to the practice of manual labor in their monasteries. Since this quickly proved unrealistic for clerical choir monks, who engaged in contemplative and liturgical prayer, study, and manuscript copying and writing, they developed the new categories of lay brothers and conversi to do the manual labor. But even this proved unrealistic for large monastic lands, so they employed lay folks in the outlying reaches of abbey property. These were overseen by lay brothers, and perhaps a priest or a choir monk. These Granges were essentially miniature monasteries where the monks would live, pray, and work for weeks or even a month before returning to the main monastery for weekly Sunday Mass and community meetings.

What does this say for us? Monasteries are places of intense and productive work! We must work too, but like the Cistercians and the Granges, we must lean on colleagues in a variety of ways to get the job done. And we must be creative in a way that works in our own day and time. It is not enough to simply repeat the past. We must build squarely on it in order to really be true to it!

A Continental Celebrity

Only a few years into his stint at Cîteaux, Bernard was sent off to found a community of his own. In 1115, at the age of only 25, he set up a monastery at Claire Vallée, later shortened to Clairvaux. By 1121 Clairvaux had already spawned three new communities itself, all while Cîteaux remained strong. The Cistercians were multiplying like rabbits!

As for Bernard, he went from being the ingenious and highly effective abbot of Clairvaux Cistercian Abbey to becoming one of the most powerful and influential voices in Europe. He wrote and preached not only to monastics but to lay leaders and common folk alike. Though like St. Bruno he never accepted a bishopric (not for lack of offers), he was nonetheless sent by popes and emperors on Church and state business. He was a master negotiator and peacemaker who inspired energetic Christianity like no one else of his time. Scholars now estimate that St. Bernard spent as much as 80% of his time outside of his abbey in ministry. Let's hope he had a great prior (or second in command) to run the place when he was gone!

This says much to us today. Spiritual leaders, preachers, and pastors must first be grounded in disciplined personal and community life in Christ and the Church. For his day that meant monastic life in a booming reformed community. For us it might mean new movements and communities. The absence of such communities attests to the shallowness of our modern approach to Catholic spirituality. Often it degenerates into legalistic categories of conservative or liberal, and usually approaches orthodoxy superficially at best. The monastic tradition takes us much, much deeper. It converts souls to a radical discipleship in Christ, and so addresses the problems of the Church and the world founded and created and redeemed by Him.

Setting the Stage for Mendicant Renewal

Lastly, the 11th century reformers set the stage for the Mendicant renewal of the 13th century that truly reshaped the Church and the Western world. The likes of St. Francis, St. Dominic, the Carmelites, and the Augustinians (just to name the main ones) might not have been possible without the reforms of the Camaldolese, the Carthusians, and the Cistercians. The semi-eremitical movement influenced the community life of early Franciscans, Carmelites, and Augustinians. The Cistercians helped Dominic form the first ministry team sent forth to combat the Cathars, who were dividing the faithful. And the insistence on a pure life based on the Gospel of Jesus Christ alone was the engine that drove them all. The preaching of not only the heavenly glorified Christ but also the human, poor, and crucified Christ signaled a change in emphasis that became the hallmark of the Mendicant movement.

What saints and movements have paved the way for our time? Are we ready to build squarely on the past to place our spiritual stone in the present, as we look towards the future in Christ and the Church?

Study Questions

1) Are we willing to pioneer new movements today? How do we relate to movements from earlier times?

2) Are we open to help and assistance from the new talent that comes to us in new inquiries and recruits?

3) Do we embrace renewal and reform that is too extreme, or are we more moderate in our expression?

4) How well do we manage the physical and fiscal dimensions of our "monastic" work?

5) Are we rooted in prayer and communal gospel life before we try to preach to others? How do we balance community and ministry in our life? How well do our spiritual leaders do so?

6) Are we willing to help and assist new movements and communities that build upon what we have already done?

CHAPTER 10: THE OPEN HANDS OF THE MENDICANTS

One of the more popular songs in my live ministry is "God Alone Is Enough," from St. Teresa of Avila. During the song I have the congregation open their hands on their laps, empty themselves of all expectations, and allow God to work His will in their lives for that evening. We try to embody Evagrius Ponticus's teaching to "renounce all to gain everything!"

St. Bonaventure wrote a book called *In Defense of the Mendicants* to defend the new orders like the Franciscans, Dominicans, Augustinians, and Carmelites from accusations from those who opposed their phenomenal growth and success in the 13th and 14th centuries. In this amazing work St. Bonaventure defines "mendicant" as being those who have no possessions, and beg with "open hands."

While most of us are not, and should not be, actual beggars, the notion of having open hands is something we can all learn from. When we open our hands we let go of our attachment to things, people, circumstances, ideas, or agendas. We release control completely to God. We are also ready to receive whatever God might fill our hands and our lives with. Are we ready to open our lives to Jesus?

The mendicants of the past devoted themselves to "the three P's": poverty, prayer, and preaching. Poverty meant to really imitate the life of Christ in radical gospel simplicity. Prayer meant living in hermitages at the outskirts of towns, where solitude and silence were really practiced in order to hear the Word of God and to live fully connected to God, creation, and the Church. Preaching meant going forth from poverty and prayer into ministry in all its forms, and often preaching more through example than words.

So let's take a look at these mendicant movements from the 13-14th centuries to see what they can teach us about our life with Christ and the Church today.

St. Francis, Dominicans, Augustinians and Carmelites

St. Francis

I have already written two books on St. Francis (*Lessons from St. Francis* and *Reflections on St. Francis*) so I could fill volumes with what I know and love about this most beloved saint. Here, I would like to limit my observations to just a few.

First, let's consider his conversion, which was not a "Saul of Tarsus" once-and-for-all conversion. In fact, it unfolded over several years, even throughout the rest of his life.

This is like most of us. Yes, there are "red letter" experiences in our conversion to Jesus, but conversions tend to unfold throughout our lives, and often build one upon one another. God reveals His will one bit at a time based on what we are ready for. If He were to give it all at once, most of us would be overwhelmed and would likely give up—or run away. Gradual conversion, on the other hand, requires faith. If we were to see God's full plan for our entire life all at once, there wouldn't be much faith required. No, He tends to lead us from one point to another by glimpses, until we can look back and see the complete picture of what He willed for us. Even for those who receive a more complete vision for their lives, the details of how it will all come to pass are left to fill in through faith. As Hebrews says, "Faith is the realization of what is hoped for and evidence of things not seen." (Heb. 11:1) And St. Paul says, "We walk by faith, not by sight." (2 Cor. 5:7)

What are the main points of St. Francis's conversion? Let's take a look at his life in a brief timeline form:

1181 – St. Francis is born and baptized under the name "John." His father, a successful cloth merchant who traded with producers in France, later takes to calling him "Francis."

1198 – Civil war hits Assisi; the people rise up and destroy the town's main fortress, the Rocca Maggiore, which represents the old feudalism of the local lord and serfs.

1202 – Francis joins the men of Assisi in a skirmish with rival Perugia, which upholds the old feudalism. The Assisians are defeated, and Francis spends a year in Perugian captivity. He begins to reconsider his worldly lifestyle.

1204 – A serious illness strikes, and another period of spiritual questioning sets in.

1204 – As he sets off for a military career, he receives a vision from God on a bridge in Apulia that makes him turn around and return to Assisi.

1205 – While praying in the derelict local chapel of San Damiano (St. Damian), Francis hears a voice saying, "Go, Francis, and repair my house, which as you see is falling into ruin." He sells some his father's silk and tries to give the money to the local priest, who rejects it. Francis scatters the gold on the street.

1206 – Francis's father takes him before the bishop, where Francis renounces his inheritance and all his possessions, flinging even the clothes on his back at his father's feet. He is clothed by the bishop himself.

1206 – Francis adopts a hermit's habit with sandals, leather cincture, and pyramidal hood.

1206 – He repairs three churches– San Damiano, San Pietro, and St. Mary of the Angels at Portiuncula – by begging people for stones and personally placing them in the church buildings.

1208 – Hearing the words from Gospel of St. Matthew in which Jesus tells his apostles to go out to the people and to "take no gold, nor silver, nor copper in your belts, no bag for your journey, nor two tunics, nor sandals, nor a staff," Francis discards his hermit's habit. He goes barefoot and wears only a scratchy tunic with a white rope belt.

1208 – Francis attracts his first brothers: Bernard of Quintavalle, Peter of Cattaneo, and Giles of Assisi. He goes into a local church and opens the Book of the Gospels to three random verses, all of which refer to giving up everything and following Christ. This, Francis announces, will be the foundation of his community.

1209 – The first rule of the Friars Minor, based on the Gospel passages mentioned above and others, is given verbal approval by Pope Innocent III. (This rule is lost to us today.)

1221 – By this time the Order had grown to thousands of brothers, so Francis decides to commit his rule to writing.

1223 – Finding the First Rule vague and confusing, Francis writes the more precise Second Rule, which is still in force to this day. The Rule of St. Francis includes vows of poverty, chastity, and obedience, with a strong emphasis on poverty. The Rule is approved by Pope Honorius III.

1224 – Francis retires from leadership in the Order as his health declines and struggles for the direction of the Order intensify. He receives the Stigmata—the five wounds of Jesus Christ—furthering the decline of his body.

1226 – Francis dies on October 3 in his old hut next to the church at Portiuncula.

Main points in Francis's conversion:

1. War with Perugia: While imprisoned in Perugia and confronted with his own mortality, Francis first begins to question his pursuit of worldly honor and acclaim.

2. Road to Apulia: Francis receives a word from God: "Francis, is it better to serve the servant or the master?" The servant is secular rulers, and the Master is God.

3. San Damiano: Not only does Francis receive an invitation from God to "repair My church," he follows through with the dilapidated church outside of Assisi. But he doesn't understand yet that God is referring to His *entire* Church.

4. Before Bishop Guido: Francis publicly disclaims his inheritance, removing himself from his wealthy family, and renounces his possessions. He is removing whatever is getting in the way of his call to holiness. The bishop clothes Francis and becomes his protector.

5. Meeting the leper: When Francis meets a leper in the street and, overcoming his revulsion, embraces him, he shows his complete trust in God and His plan.

We can see that even Francis's initial conversion took around six years! It really took from 1202 to 1208 for his vision of the Order of Friars Minor to come together. And from there it continued to unfold over the course of his life. Most of his conversions were coupled with struggle, apparent failure, and trial. But these challenges led to greater success in a way Francis would not have found otherwise.

We should be able to relate to this. We often have to grope in the dark a bit, or even a lot, to find out what God wants for us. Yes, we want to follow Jesus. We want to give our life completely to Him. But discovering the "how" takes time, trial, and error. St. Francis reminds us to stay faithful through that often frustrating process. God really does have a wonderful plan for each one of our lives, and each one is unlike anyone else's.

There are three essential aspects to the Franciscan way, as we previously mentioned: poverty, prayer, and preaching.

Poverty

One of the most incredible and misunderstood aspects of the spirituality and practice of St. Francis is his complete refusal to use or even touch money, except in the case of helping the poor. Otherwise, the brothers were strictly forbidden to come into contact with it! This is clear throughout his words and his extant Rules, and the biographies confirm this teaching.

It helps to place this restriction in the context of contemporary continental Europe. During the time of Francis there was a socioeconomic shift occurring from a predominantly barter economy, with the use of coins only to augment transactions, to the almost exclusive use of money for trade and business. The world of Francis had gone wild for money!

This was compounded by the shift from the feudal system to a more democratic society. In the feudal system serfs would remain poor for generations and would rarely travel anywhere outside their region. The feudal lord would travel on behalf of the region he governed. In the more democratic system, one could rise from poverty (*minore*, or minors) to wealth (*maggiore*, or majors) through hard work, and travel extensively for business. The world of Francis was truly on the move, both culturally and geographically!

Francis's own father, Pietro Bernardone, had made this transition from poor to rich, having even married into a family of *maggiore* through Lady Pica, his wife. But even with all these amazing revolutions unfolding in his family, Francis perceived that his father was still an unhappy, even greedy man. Francis longed for something more.

Francis found that "something more" by founding and living in an order based on his experience of radically following the Gospel of Jesus—one in which he could intentionally choose to remain a "minor" for life and never touch money, while still being happier than those who were intoxicated with the cultural revolution going on around him. Francis cut through the false promises of economics and politics, and found lasting wealth and God's eternal kingdom by radically renouncing it all to follow the way of Jesus Christ as closely as possible. Francis's poverty was never poverty for the sake of poverty. It was always gospel poverty, or a poverty that flowed from and led back to a relationship with Jesus Christ.

The example of Francis compels all those who seek to follow Jesus radically to examine how we might still get caught up in the worlds of politics and economics. Sometimes we place more hope in the things of this world than we realize; we think we have renounced them until they are threatened, and then we discover how frightened or angry we might become. Sometimes we are so encumbered by these things that we rarely, if ever, really break free to live the Gospel of Jesus Christ as our deepest heart longs to.

Today, we often get caught up in the new economy of credit. It is the allure of "easy spending" that has caused many to lose their life savings—and their soul. We are consumed by what we consume, and possessed by our possessions. This has been exacerbated through social media where the simple touch of a button enables us to purchase rooms of stuff without even leaving our homes. I think Francis would encourage a slower process of spending so that we would really think about why we spend before doing so. As a prophetic statement he might forbid today's mendicants to use credit cards at all.

Likewise, some place more hope in politics than in Jesus. While appropriate political involvement is good, it remains secondary for the Catholic Christian. We are far too familiar with those who obviously or subtly make politics their primary expression of religion, from the Islamic extremist to the fanatically political Christian. When we do not have a strong sense of the Church we often project that need onto a secular government. It ends in frustration and anger that unnecessarily destroys peace. St. Francis radically challenges this all too popular polarizing phenomenon.

What about us? What is the "money" that distracts us today? Is it easy spending through credit cards and online shopping? Is it addiction to social media? Or perhaps we have subtly replaced the Gospel with a preoccupation with politics? Francis prophetically reminds us of the limitations of these otherwise valid worldly pursuits.

Prayer

But poverty was not the whole of St. Francis's spirituality. It was rooted deeply in prayer, and overflowed into ministry. In fact, like St.

Paul, Jesus, and the Apostles, poverty was only a means to dependence on God, and to a complete freedom to minister anywhere in the world without encumbrance.

While we often think of Francis in relation to gospel poverty and evangelization, he also founded over 20 hermitages in his lifetime. This is remarkable! These hermitages were the bases of prayer and simple living from which his ministry of almost boundless energy went forth.

Again, this must be placed in some historical context. In response to the cultural shifts already mentioned, as well as great abuses and lapses in the Church, many groups large and small were popping up all across Europe. Some were orthodox, and some strayed into schism or heresy. Some were effective and popular, and some were not. Some outlived their initial success, but most did not.

These groups often gathered in a new semi-eremitical pattern and overflowed into ministry. Scholars now say that Mount Subasio, above Francis's home town of Assisi, was pockmarked with such hermitages.

Francis's original way of life was one of wandering, or itinerancy, in imitation of Jesus and the apostles. But his order quickly discovered that they needed some stable places to lay their heads between ministries. For Francis these places took the form of hermitages on the outskirts of the towns where they ministered. It was simply part of the spiritual movement of the time.

Cardinal Jacques de Vitry, a cardinal who was very interested in guiding new communities and movements, described the Friars' way of life as an alternation among contemplative prayer in hermitages, apostolic ministry to the poor in towns, and preaching to the masses.

Francis's *Rule for Those Who live in Hermitages* describes three or four friars living in a hermitage. Half lived in strict solitude, and the rest took care of the domestic needs of the hermitage, including daily begging in the nearby village or town. They would trade places as the Spirit led, so that all of them served and prayed intensely in this eremitical environment. This pattern is repeated, often with 10-15 friars, but always with this alteration of solitude and community service.

That this was so ordinary is demonstrated by the fact that both St. Anthony of Padua and St. Bonaventure lived in hermitages. St. Anthony had come from the Augustinian Clerics and had hidden his clerical ordination by living as a lay brother in a hermitage. It was only after he was forced to preach when a visiting cardinal was there that anyone discovered that he was not only ordained, but highly educated and the best preacher anyone had ever heard. St. Bonaventure legendarily received his cardinal's hat while washing dishes in a hermitage, and had them hang it on the tree outside—an image that ended up on his coat of arms!

The great 20th century Franciscan scholar Kajetan Esser pointed out that Francis stood firmly in the tradition of the great hermitage dwellers among the Desert Fathers, changing only the extent of his cloister. Francis's community was immediately international, and required a whole new leadership structure to accommodate a community that was not limited to one single monastery. He said, "The world is my cloister, my body is my cell, and my soul is the hermit within."

Do we really ground ourselves in prayer before trying to minister? Francis said, "I seek not so much to pray, but to become a prayer." But this never became an excuse for failing to set aside times and places for intense contemplative prayer. Francis made communal and private prayer primary before reaching out in ministry. Only when we intentionally set aside definite times and places for prayer does our whole life become a prayer, as Francis said. Otherwise we cop out of prayer and begin to treat our ministry as if it is part of our personal identity, burning out when we run out of spiritual gas. As I have often taught, your ministry must flow from your being in Christ; your being cannot be focused on ministry. Otherwise we often suffocate the ministries that are supposed to be directed by God, and spiritually burn ourselves out in the process!

Preaching

As the world became more mobile through international merchant travel, Francis's new community became mobile, and brothers were often assigned to many houses in their lifetime. Some traveled extensively instead of staying in one monastery for most of their life. His new community became a true order, living and preaching under one centralized leadership throughout the world.

"Preach at all times, and if necessary use words." This quote is often attributed to St. Francis, and fairly represents his spirituality, though he never said it explicitly. The fact remains: Preaching included a way of life, acts of mercy for those in need, and at times, for those with the gift and ordination, to preach informally or formally.

Francis's lifestyle was so radical that it preached louder than words. His life focused not just on general care for the poor, but specifically care for lepers, those most shunned by society. It also included times for lay preaching of general penance, or conversion to Christ, or of doctrine in the case of clerics. But have no doubt, all these forms of preaching were given a new power from the Spirit of God stirred up through a radical gospel life!

What does this all say for us? We must also find a prayer base from which to minister to others. We must set aside times and places for more intense solitary and communal prayer, and overflow from that into an entire way of life that preaches the Gospel of Jesus Christ with the power of the Spirit.

Do we realize that we preach by our entire way of life? Pope Francis says in *The Joy of the Gospel* that our whole life becomes a gospel, or good message! We do it by living a life of newfound joy in Jesus.

The Poor Ladies of St. Clare

I will not attempt to give a full account of St. Clare's life and spirituality, but some mention must be made of this astonishing woman of God. She represents the female counterpart to the male example of St. Francis, and no understanding of the Franciscan movement is complete without her.

The lifestyle and preaching of Francis didn't just inspire men. He also inspired women who wanted to embrace the Gospel of Jesus Christ in the way that he preached and lived. The first of these was St. Clare. She was struck to the core by the Gospel Francis preached and lived, and she wanted to join him.

But how could she join a new fledgling community of men? Being of a *maggiore* aristocratic family, Clare had to covertly run away to join this new, untried expression of Francis and his first brothers. She had to literally sneak out in the night through the door only used for carrying out the dead from a typical house in Assisi. This door is literally called the "death door"! What an apt sign! She had to die to her old way of life in order to discover a new way of life preached by Francis in Jesus Christ.

But what could Francis do with one woman? Francis put her in the care of some nearby Benedictine nuns for initial formation. Like Francis, the first obstacle that St. Clare faced was her father. He really didn't know what to do with her. He didn't support her in the decision to join Francis, so he personally went to the convent to get her out. But it was too late. She had already shorn her hair and donned the habit and veil of one consecrated completely to God. Upon his appearance she simply removed her veil to reveal that her ample and beautiful locks of golden hair had been shorn in the style of a nun. She was already consecrated to God in the eyes of the Church, and so he had to resign himself to her decision. Soon others followed, including her sister, and her mother! A community was being born!

She embraced a way of life more poor and secluded in the enclosure of the cloister than what was normal even for cloistered sisters of her day. And she required no dowry to pay for the expenses from prospective members. This was radical in a way beyond what we can quite imagine in our culture where women are generally self-sufficient and often professionals in their own right. The dowry was paid by the family to economically support the prospective sister (or bride in marriage for that matter) for a good part of their natural life. Like Francis, she didn't even touch money.

She wanted to hold nothing back, embracing the ancient but novel preaching of Francis in a way adapted to sisters in a strict contemplative cloister. It was radical and revolutionary. The next obstacle she faced was the very Church to whom she was so devoted.

The Church did not share her zeal. They counseled moderation and wanted her to accept money, and to not be so strictly cloistered. This was not unloving, or because they resisted her calling. They just wanted it to succeed through greater moderation. The Church, therefore, imposed Benedictine Constitutions on her new community. She obeyed, but continued to humbly submit her own Rule based on the Franciscan Rule of the Order of Friars Minor. Permission to live by her Rule was still not granted, but she persevered in humility and obedience until just weeks before she died, when the Church allowed her rule to be used for the convent of San Damiano just outside of Assisi. After many years the entire Order of St. Clare was finally permitted to follow her Rule.

Clare's community was overtly monastic, not made up of mendicant wanderers like Francis and the brothers. At that time the idea of women wandering as itinerant hermits and preachers was simply unheard of. And there was a good reason for this: It was unsafe! There were robbers and brigands on most of the roads in those days. So women interested in a consecrated life had to settle in monasteries that were securely locked away and safe. Clare was no different.

Clare is known for many wonderful things, of which I will mention only a few more in passing.

The story of her removing the Eucharist when Assisi was threatened with Muslim invasion is legendary, and depicted in many paintings and holy cards. (The Muslim incursion into Christian Europe was real, and most threatening to Christianity.) Some say that she stood atop the monastery of San Damiano and bravely faced down the attackers with only the Eucharist, and they fled in confusion. Most scholars believe that she was simply removing the Sacrament to a safe place when the attackers appeared, and the sight of her sent them into retreat. Either way, the sisters were spared by a supernatural force of God in connection to the Eucharist!

Clare was also very sick in her final years. She could not move from her simple mat on the floor in the common one-room dormitory above the church. Day after day she lay on her mat and prayed. During community prayers and Mass she would participate by gazing through a little door they had cut through the floor by her mat looking through the ceiling of the church. To this day they keep a single flower where she lay in holy prayer day after day until her death.

Last, but not least, Clare was the woman of Lady Poverty. Scholars of Franciscana, or "things Franciscan," now see that her writings are even more filled with a zeal for poverty than were the writings of St. Francis! It seems unbelievable, but it is true! Francis tended to emphasize obedience even before poverty, and as the greatest expression of poverty of spirit. But in her ardent desire to follow the Rule of the Order of Friars Minor, she emphasized poverty even more. This was her unique contribution to the spirituality and organization of women's cloistered communities.

The Third Order: A Lay Revolution

St. Francis attracted serious followers not only from celibate men and women, the religious, and the clergy, but also from average folks in the secular world. Countless couples were inspired to embrace the Franciscan message in a way appropriate to their state of life. Francis accommodated this through his "Third Order," originally called simply The Order of Penance, and now called The Secular Franciscan Order. Using the language of a "first, second, and third order" from the popular, yet heretical Cathars, Francis enabled secular folks to join him in his prayer, mission, and preaching.

This eventually resulted in a Rule of Life that included all aspects of life in way appropriate to their secular state. However, there is one important exception: The Rule prohibited taking up arms in any form. This was revolutionary. Third Order Franciscans became a peaceful movement that swept through every level of secular life. Most scholars now say that a substantial peace movement spread across Europe at this time as the elite of society refused to take up arms in imitation of Jesus Christ. The typical wars that plagued Europe simply stopped.

The Third Order also became a place where further expressions of religious life were birthed. Today this is generally called the Third Order Regular. For instance, communities of consecrated women dedicated to active works were established by the Spirit as the wider society became able to support them, whereas previously it was considered too dangerous for women to be so active in a culture where violence and force prevailed. As organizational problems and divisions began to fracture the Order of Friars Minor, new examples of the hermitage for simple brothers also rose up. Francis had prophesied that as friars threw off their habits and went back into the world, lay people would pick up their habits and go into the hermitage with greater love and zeal than ever before. As one Franciscan scholar, Alan Wolter, OFM, said, "The cloister went out into the world, and the world was brought back into the cloister."

Study Questions

1)   Do we empty and open our life of all so that we can gain everything in Christ?

2)   What are the "three P's," and how do they work in our life?

3)   Do we allow our conversion to unfold over time, or do we feel frustrated because we do not see our whole life clearly from the beginning?

4)   Do we set aside intentional times of solitude and silence for prayer?

5)   Do we see our entire life as a gospel, and understand that we are preaching in everything that we do?

6)   How do we see cloistered women and a purely contemplative life as important in the Church?

7)   Are we who are in the secular world really inspired by the Franciscan ideal to evangelize the entire world for Jesus Christ?

St. Dominic

I have always been considered pretty much a Franciscan in my spiritual expression of the more general monastic life. That is true, but when I took one particular Myers-Briggs personality test, it said I would make an ideal Dominican! Boy, was I surprised! Then again, on reflection it wasn't so surprising. Dominic Guzman founded a contemplative order of prayer and serious study overflowing into apostolic preaching. That's pretty much what I do too, except I preach through music, teaching, and lay preaching. Yes, I must confess that, while relatively little is known about St. Dominic, I love him as a spiritual elder in my integrated monastic life.

A quick anecdote about my connection with the Dominicans: When I was beginning my journey into Catholicism, I was given a Catholic cross by a friend who revealed that he was an ordained priest in a Coptic-related church under an African bishop. I was surprised, but accepted the gift with love. Later I found out that it was a Dominican Cross!

There are a few stories about the brotherhood shared between Francis and Dominic.

One story is that Dominic was visiting during the Chapter of Mats, where the Franciscans would meet around the Portiuncula Chapel and hermitage below Assisi. There were some 5,000 brothers gathered there, living in temporary huts and makeshift tents. They prayed, listened to teaching from Francis and others, and discussed their life and mission together. But they didn't supply any food! They relied on God to take care of them.

Dominic remarked that this was a serious oversight, and mentioned it to Francis. Francis said they lived in gospel poverty, and relied on God to supply their needs. Dominic began sharing about the need for wisdom in applying such scriptures too literally. About that time the townspeople from Assisi began streaming from town with ample supplies for the Friars and their guests.

Dominic was stunned, and from that time forward embraced mendicant poverty more radically than he had proposed. It changed his direction and that of his Order of Preachers markedly, and made them more successful than before.

Another story is that Dominic and Francis became such close friends that Dominic proposed that they merge their orders into one community for greater effectiveness. Francis listened with joy, but wisely corrected Dominic that God had inspired them as brothers to found two orders for two different, but complementary communities. Dominic agreed, but he asked for Francis's cord, which he reverently wore beneath his Dominican habit until he died. Despite years and even decades of theological differences around the emphasis on St. Thomas Aquinas and St. Bonaventure (who were also friends) by those who followed these two great theological doctors of the Church, the Dominicans and Franciscans have considered themselves as spiritual cousins.

This has much to teach us today! Often when I visit parishes I am astounded at the polarization that exists among the numerous ministries and small groups. Diverse ethnic, linguistic, and spiritual backgrounds are gifts. But when they become excuses for division and withdrawal from the greater parish in major ministries where the entire parish gathers together, they are no longer instruments of God, but obstacles to the work of God. Small groups are meant to strengthen the entire parish. But when they compete, or are jealous when another group does well or offers something for the entire parish or diocese, there is clearly something wrong! Yet, this often proves to be the case. That is why we demand that on the nights of my Catholic Revivals all small group parish activity be cancelled, and we all gather together as one community in communion in Christ.

Life of St. Dominic

St. Dominic Guzman was born in 1170 in the Castilian region of Spain. From an early age he became known for his seriousness and studiousness; he excelled in all his learning. After successfully running some errands for the King of Castile—namely negotiating a marriage arrangement with a distant princess!—Dominic and some friends traveled to Rome in the hope of getting approval to go on far flung missions.

Providence—and the pope—had a different idea. Dominic was instead sent to the south of France to combat the Cathar heresy (more on this below). It was here that Dominic really caught the preaching bug. He would challenge Cathar leaders to public theological disputations, or debates, where he would consistently defeat them in pitched intellectual battle. This talent, in combination with his clearly humble and ascetic lifestyle, won many souls back to orthodox Catholicism.

As Dominic's reputation spread he was asked multiple times to become a bishop, but he never had a taste for church administration. He'd rather be out in the field preaching the Gospel of Jesus Christ. God had bigger things in store for him, as well.

It turned out that at this time, around the year 1215, the Church was actively looking for innovative ways to attack the problem of heresies popping up around Europe. Enter St. Dominic's charism for preaching. While the Church was initially opposed to approving any new religious orders, when Dominic proposed that his new order of preachers would use the already-existing Augustinian Rule the Church dropped its objection. Dominic was then made Master of the Sacred Palace, now called Theologian of the Pontifical Household or simply Pope's Theologian, an office that has been held by a Dominican friar for 800 years.

With the strong support of Rome, the Order of Friars Preachers, as it is called, grew considerably and is credited with smothering many popular heresies. Dominic personally founded countless friaries and convents throughout Europe before his death from illness, exacerbated by exhaustion, in 1221, at the age of 51.

Cistercians Help in First Mission

An interesting aspect of Dominic's ministry is his connection with the Cistercians. (Remember them from our previous chapter including St. Bernard of Clairvaux?) When Dominic started his preaching mission he didn't have a community to join with him. He turned to the contemplative Cistercians for help. They were the most numerous and powerful community in the Western Church, and had already overflowed from contemplation into apostolic mission, so it was a logical choice.

At first it was five Cistercians who joined Dominic for his mission of apostolic preaching from a foundation of contemplative prayer and theological study. As men began to join Dominic the Cistercians went back to their communities. Dominic went on to found his community as a centralized religious order with an international scope under one common superior.

Order of Preachers

Dominic's vision was simple. He originally envisioned a double community: one for contemplative sisters and one for men who would preach. (Remember that the world was still too dangerous and violent for women to engage in direct ministry outside of protected cloisters.) Both were rooted in prayer and study of Scripture, but the women would be the active prayer warriors for the Friars, who would be out in the dangers of the world preaching. As it turned out this double model was not always possible, but the importance of prayer, study, and preaching has remained basic to the Dominican charism.

While St. Francis founded an Order of Friars Minor that emphasized gospel poverty while also preaching, Dominic founded an Order of Preachers that emphasized preaching ahead of living a life of gospel simplicity.

There were two schismatic and/or heretical communities that were growing quickly and tearing simple people away from the orthodoxy of the Catholic Church: the Cathars and the Waldensians. Dominic intentionally tried to combat the Cathars, a community that embraced poverty, but out of a dualistic belief that the created world was evil. Francis focused on the Waldensians, who emphasized poverty in contrast to an often rich and corrupt Catholic clergy and ended at first in schism (or division from the Church without affecting doctrine), but later led their more extreme followers into doctrinal heresy.

Both Dominic and Francis championed an orthodox approach to correcting the excesses of a corrupt clergy. They sought to live radical gospel poverty as much as, or even more than, the schismatic and heretical groups breaking away from the Church. Further, they preached not only with powerful words, but through the integrity of a radical gospel lifestyle. And both Dominic and Francis succeeded!

Who are the Cathars and Waldensians of our day? Let me interject: I would say that it is the mega church movement! I often hear Catholics bemoan that mega churches are "stealing our children!" But I would rather ask, why are they able to be stolen? And, what might they be doing right, albeit from an incomplete or erroneous theological perspective, that we might learn from, fully baptize, and use in our Catholic Faith as we bring the Gospel of Jesus Christ from the ancient path to folks in our own culture today?

Only 17% of Catholics in America are still coming to church. And only 15% of our youth are still coming to church! If it were a denomination, the second largest denomination in America would be non-practicing Catholics; there's 30 million of them! And a large number of the folks in the mega church pews down the street are non-practicing Catholics! Now they don't leave to get away from the sacraments, good balanced teaching, or the countless works of mercy done daily by the Church for those most needy in our midst. They go because they find engaged worship and aggressively welcoming communities elsewhere.

Pope Francis says, "I invite every Christian, at this very moment, to a renewed personal encounter with Jesus Christ!" Now that's the engagement we need! You can't give what you don't have. You can't evangelize until you have been evangelized! It is encounter with Jesus Christ that empowers engagement in liturgies and faith communities!

And it's not rocket science, folks! We need better worship music, and better preaching of God's Word in Catholic parishes across America. When we prepare people with better worship music that encourages them to actually pray and sing, and better preaching of God's Word that stirs their faith, then we are ready for a personal encounter with Jesus Christ in every Eucharist that is personal, intimate, and life-changing. Then, every Eucharist becomes an altar call where we come forward to give our life to Christ fully as His disciples. He gave His life for us 2,000 years ago, and re-enacts and extends that one unrepeatable saving act sacramentally on the altar at every Mass!

Dominic and Francis call us from our ancient past to bring real Catholic revival today! America needs revival now! And this begins in our parishes, and in every human heart. Let's bring that revival one parish at a time, and one human heart at a time. Then we can see the whole world revived in Jesus Christ!

Study Questions

1) Are we able to work with other groups or movements in the Church to bring the Gospel of Jesus Christ to our secular humanist world?

2) Do we embrace gospel simplicity according to our own state of life to give integrity to our various ministries?

3) Do we base our ministry on prayer, or burn out by ministering without real spiritual fuel?

4)   Do we engage in adequate study of Scripture and theology, such as Lectio Divina, before we try to preach to
others?

5)   5)   What are some of the breakaway groups of our era,
and how do we reach out to them to re-establish unity
and reform in the Church?

Augustinians

I first encountered the Augustinians when I did a concert in the field
house at Villanova outside Philadelphia. During those days I stayed
with the Augustinian friars, who were wonderful and welcomed me
with great hospitality! I greatly enjoyed a fruitful dialogue about
what I was doing in the eremitical Franciscan tradition, and how that
related to the Augustinian tradition. They showed me resources for
study that I thoroughly enjoyed and greatly benefitted from.

When we think of Augustinians we naturally think of St. Augustine.
But that's not really the way it happened! The successful monastic
movement of St. Augustine died out quickly after the invasion of
the barbarians into Northern Africa. But his Rule remained a prized
treasure in monastic literature.

The Augustinians we think of actually date back to the Augustinian
Clerics of the pre-mendicant era, as well as the Order of St.
Augustine, which arose from a scattering of hermit communities
that consolidated into a bona fide religious orders as part of the
mendicant movement.

It's a story not unlike the beginnings of what we today call the Third
Order Regular Franciscans. Isolated groups of hermits living a poor
and radical gospel life struggled to survive on their own. Some discovered each other on their own, and some were brought together

by a concerned member of the Church hierarchy, and were united into an Order.

While the Order began as hermits, they became mendicants through the Grand Union, which united groups of hermits dedicated to Augustine and St. William the Hermit, and began to engage the local people though begging and ministry. The Williamites eventually left the Union over this development, and embraced the Benedictine Rule. Nevertheless, this union laid the groundwork for the development of the esteemed Order of St. Augustine we know today. The semi-eremitical beginnings, consolidation of several smaller communities into one larger one, and overflowing into ministry is what I find appealing.

I must admit a great love for the Rule of St. Augustine, and I have a great love for the origins of the modern Order of St. Augustine. I pray that this very brief description will cause you to investigate them for yourself at greater length.

Carmelites

I first encountered Carmelites in Munster, Indiana, long before I was Catholic. They are a Polish community that left their homeland to escape persecution. The locals in Munster take pride in the grounds of the monastery, where rock from Poland has been used to erect a series of prayer walks and grottos that are a true jewel of the area. Of course, I knew nothing of the Catholic Church or the Carmelites. I only knew that the monastery and grounds were holy, and that the brothers seemed to walk with an incredible air of contemplative peace that affected my searching spirit and soul on a deep level.

It was later that I discovered Carmelites in a more personal way. First, I met the sisters at the Carmel in Indianapolis. I used to provide music for Masses celebrated by Fr. Martin Wolter, OFM—my

Franciscan director. They were holy, but truly fun, and not a little funny! Since then I have delighted in visiting Carmelite convents across the world, and always find them holy, pure, and joyful!

It was in Ireland that I encountered the Friars again. At Gort Muire, or the Field of Mary, retreat center outside of Dublin I met Fr. John Keating and Fr. Christopher O'Donnell, the liaison for the Catholic Charismatic Renewal. Fr. Chris is the one who encouraged me to put St. Teresa's Prayer, "Christ Has No Body, But Yours," to music. But it was also there that I was introduced to the ancient Carmelite Rule.

I was surprised to discover that it is the only canonical semi-ere-mitical rule in the Christian West! Yes, there are semi-eremitical and eremitical constitutions, as with the Carthusians, Camaldolese, or Franciscans, but this is the only semi-eremitical *rule* in the Western Church!

From there my mind raced back to my visits to Mount Carmel above present day Haifa, Israel, where I had visited the cave over which the Carmelite church is built. I soon discovered the nearby valley where the remains of their first hermitages were discovered. No wonder I had always felt such a kindred spirit with the Carmelites! I was called to live in the hermitage and overflow into ministry, and so were they, right from the origins of their community!

Apparently many crusaders gave up their military life and embraced a purely eremitical life on Mount Haifa, in a safe zone for Christians. Their numbers grew, so they sought permission to establish a way of life from Albert, the Bishop of Jerusalem. Extraordinarily, he ended up giving them the only semi-eremitical rule to survive in the Roman Catholic Church in the West.

It is a rather standard rule, but clearly retains the semi-eremitical dimension in their way of life, outlining that they are to be hermits in individual and separated cells. They are to have a prior who resides near the gate to the hermitages, to pray the Divine Office and celebrate Mass together daily, and to eat together to ensure a sense of community and the health of their members.

This seemed to work well for quite some time. But these hermits did not live in a peaceful and secure land. The crusades were in full swing, and the territory of Christians and Muslims ebbed and flowed. Soon Muslims threatened Mount Carmel, and the hermits sought refuge in Italy. They were welcomed, but were encouraged to embrace the new mendicant way of life that was sweeping Italy and Europe at the time. It seemed a good idea, so the Carmelites did so, using their hermitages as bases for ministry among the people.

From there the order did what most orders do. It succeeded, then grew fat and sluggish, and then needed occasional reform. The greatest of all reforms is known as the Teresian Reform in Spain, which produced St. Teresa of Avila and St. John of the Cross. As marvelous as this reform was, it did not fully rediscover the semi-er-emitical dimension of their original life. It was cenobitical, or fra-ternal. The reform re-established their houses as radical places of prayer and poverty, but only occasionally allowed for the hermit way of life.

I have a great love for all things eremitical and monastic, and I have a special love for the Carmelites, who have such a strong semi-ere-mitical foundation. I pray with and for them all in the Spirit today as they seek to apply that life and spirituality in the great challenges of living in the secular humanist West. Just as the hermits of Mount Carmel had to adapt in order to meet the challenges of the Muslim onslaught, so we must all adapt to our dissolute modern culture.

I think it appropriate also to mention our Christian brothers and sisters who are being persecuted and martyred by radical and extremist Muslims in the Middle East today. The Carmelites met this challenge in their own time, and managed to continue on with great success. We must encourage those facing the same challenges, including offering refuge in ways that retain the traditions of each Eastern Christian community being persecuted and martyred today.

Study Questions

1) Can we see a repeating theme of independent hermitages and unions in Church history, and apply it to our own situation today?

2) Are we able to join with other movements and communities to accomplish something greater than we can do alone?

3) Do we value our origins, while also recognizing that we sometimes need reform?

4) Are we able to reform in a way that is effective in a new setting and environment?

5) How can we adapt the ancient roots of monasticism to our secular humanist West?

6) How can we offer refuge and protection to our Eastern Christian brothers and sisters suffering persecution and martyrdom from extremist Muslims today?

CHAPTER 11: EASTERN CHRISTIAN MONASTICISM

I often use a song called "Breathe" in my ministries to get people ready for The Jesus Prayer, a rosary-like contemplative prayer from the Christian East. I explain that the words for "spirit" in both Hebrew (*ruah*) and Greek (*pneuma*) mean "air, wind, and breath." I teach them to unite every breath they take with the wonderful beauty of the Spirit of God.

St. John Paul II once used the Pauline analogy that the Church is the body of Christ, and like anybody she has two lungs—a Western lung and an Eastern lung. I actually have folks grab their two lungs and breathe deeply. The problem is that we have only been breathing from one lung—the Western lung!

Most folks attending my ministries are either Latin (also known as Roman) Rite Catholics or are from a faith community that traces itself to the Protestant Reformation, which emerged out of Western Europe. So most people I minister to are breathing from the Western lung!

This means that we are not really getting a full breath of the Holy Spirit in our Church life. If we want a full breath of the Spirit we need to breathe from both lungs!

Most folks don't know that there are over twenty liturgical rites and communities in the Catholic Church. Out of these many rites, only one is the well-known Latin Rite. Most of the remaining ones are Eastern rites!

This mirrors how the Catholic Church was founded and grew. In the early Church there were originally 4 major patriarchates, or diocesan centers that nurtured apostolic antiquity: Jerusalem in the land of Jesus and the first apostles, Antioch where Paul and Peter ministered, Alexandria in Egypt where Mark the Apostle labored, and Rome where Paul and Peter died. Later, when the Roman Empire divided into a Western and Eastern empire, Constantinople was added as "the new Rome."

Now this doesn't mean that we are supposed to switch liturgical rites. In fact, only those with ethnic ties to an Eastern rite, or those coming into the Church, may choose an Eastern rite. But, we can and should share a working knowledge of one another's liturgical traditions.

Plus, there is the monastic history, which grew from the East towards the West. As we have seen in previous chapters, the entire monastic movement grew from primitive beginnings around Eastern churches, really bloomed in Egypt, and spread West from there.

This study brought a deep love and appreciation for the Eastern monastic expressions that survive and prosper today. Whether it be Coptic monasticism from Egypt, Maronite monks from Lebanon, or Greek or Russian monastic expressions, I appreciate them all, and have learned invaluable lessons from each that enrich my life as a member of the Brothers and Sisters of Charity, a new integrated monastic expression.

The lessons are enough to fill volumes, and we have already studied some of them in past chapters, so I will focus only on a few that I believe can help every Christian today.

Cross Bearers and Spirit Bearers

Pope St. John Paul II wrote beautifully of the connection between the cross and bearing the Spirit in Eastern Monasticism.

> In this way, by becoming bearers of the Cross (*staurophoroi*), they have striven to become bearers of the Spirit (*pneumatophoroi*), authentically spiritual men and women, capable of endowing history with hidden fruitfulness by unceasing praise and intercession, by spiritual counsels and works of charity. In its desire to transfigure the world and life itself in expectation of the definitive vision of God's countenance, Eastern monasticism gives pride of place to conversion, self-renunciation and compunction of heart, the quest for hesychia or interior peace, ceaseless prayer, fasting and vigils, spiritual combat and silence, Paschal joy in the presence of the Lord and the expectation of his definitive coming, and the oblation of self and personal possessions, lived in the holy communion of the monastery or in the solitude of the hermitage. (Pope John Paul II, *Vita Consecrata* (Consecrated Life), 1996)

St. Paul speaks of this in scripture when he says, "In contrast, the fruit of the Spirit is love, joy, peace, patience, kindness, generosity, faithfulness, gentleness, self-control. Against such there is no law. Now those who belong to Christ have crucified their flesh with its passions and desires. If we live in the Spirit, let us also follow the Spirit." (Gal. 5:22-25)

The monks of the Christian East teach us about how to be bearers of the cross so we might really become bearers of the Spirit.

But how does this actually happen? They give us disciplines that help us to be open both to the way of the cross, and to the anointing of the Holy Spirit.

Hesychasm

The contemplative monks of the East are often called *"hesychasts."* The word is most often translated as, "sacred stillness." It is found in Scripture, and the biblical Greek is ήσυχία (*hesychia*) meaning "stillness," i.e. desistance from bustle or language.

St. Paul uses the word when he speaks of a life of peace and quiet: "We hear that some are conducting themselves among you in a disorderly way, by not keeping busy but minding the business of others. Such people we instruct and urge in the Lord Jesus Christ to *work quietly* and to eat their own food." (2 Thess. 3:11-12)

In the monastic tradition it means to silence the body through a particular prayer posture and to still the breath by uniting it to the Jesus Prayer, so that the unruly thoughts and emotions settle down and we are able to focus on the things of God again. Jesus remains the focus. Everything else is only a tool to help us focus on Him.

The monastics use several analogies to illustrate this.

The first is that of a pond. If the waters of a pond are agitated, they stir up the mud at the bottom and cause the water to become murky. You cannot really see into the pond when the waters are cloudy and troubled. Likewise, the surface, which can beautifully reflect an image when still, is now only able to reflect at best a fractured image. You have to let the pond settle for a while before it is stilled, and you can see clearly into the waters again. Plus, it can once more reflect a beautiful image when the waters are calm.

This is like our soul. The waters of the pond of our soul are often agitated by the world. Thoughts become unfocused, and emotions become unruly and out of control. We can no longer see what God is doing in our soul when the waters are clouded. Plus, we cannot really reflect a complete image of God. We reflect a fractured image at best, or maybe we lose the ability to reflect an image at all. When we settle down through *hesychia* our body, breath, emotions, and thoughts become focused and clear again. The constant movement of the often-jerky and -aching body becomes smooth. Our breath is calm and even. Our emotions settle down. Then our mind becomes is clear and focused.

The mind, emotions, breath, and senses of the body never stop. If they did, you'd be dead! But they can be used rightly through sacred stillness. When they are used rightly we use the mind to have the mind of Christ. Emotions no longer enable negativity, but empower godly things through godly enthusiasm. The breath constantly unites us with the Spirit of God and the person of Jesus Christ. And the body becomes the vehicle through which our spiritual life is lived in the created world.

Watchfulness

The mind cannot cease to think, but it can be calm and focused. This is called "watchfulness," or *nepsis* (νεπσις) in Greek. In the Eastern monastic tradition, which means to be constantly aware of what is happening in our soul. Unlike scrupulosity, which is obsessive and makes us uptight, nervous, and destroys our peace, watchfulness brings a great peace to the soul.

The thoughts are sometimes called the *logizomai* (λογῐζομαι) in Scripture, and the Eastern fathers speak of thoughts as *logismoi*. They rightly observe that we process everything with thoughts, so the thoughts can be tools for good or evil in the spiritual life. As we have seen in previous chapters, the monastic tradition believes that, while the Devil and his demons cannot make you sin, they can tempt you by placing thoughts into your mind. If we give into them, the body and/or ego are stimulated, and we soon act on the tempting thoughts and stimulations.

The Steps of Temptation

This leads us easily into the Eastern monastic treatment of the steps of temptation. In the East they often speak of five to seven, or even nine well-defined steps. These are most insightful. But for myself, I find this too much to remember "on the fly!" I prefer the threefold steps offered by St. Augustine earlier:

1) *Temptation*: This is where a thought of sin simply enters the mind. But it is not yet sin. It is only temptation.

2) *Entertaining thoughts*: This is where we begin to play with our thoughts, and let them seriously entice us through our own weaknesses, often established by past sin. This is not yet the external act of sin, but it is sin internally. This is where greed, lust, and the like are active.

3) *The action of sin*: This is external sin in earnest. We either say or do actions of sin. This can also include the seemingly passive acts of misusing TV, radio, or social media. But don't be deceived! These things are sin. They are actions.

The Spider and the Web

The Eastern Hesychasts use the example of a spider and a web to illustrate sacred stillness and watchfulness. The active work of weaving a web is like the active Christian life of virtue, asceticism, and positive meditation on the Word of God. After the active work of weaving a web the spider becomes completely still in order to perceive any motion caused by prey getting caught in the web. This is like discerning thoughts, emotions, or carnal stirrings in your soul in contemplative *hesychia*. Once perceived, they can be properly discerned as being from God, self, or the Devil, and can be dealt with as positive or negative things in our life with God. The things of God are positive, human thoughts are neutral, and devilish temptations are evil.

Cutting Off the Snake's Head

Another interesting example of dealing with thoughts is the somewhat gruesome image of cutting off a snake's head. In this case, though, we are dealing with negative thoughts. This example says that it's easier to cut off the head of a serpent when only the head is in the doorway of the house of the soul than when the entire body is in the house. If the entire body gets in, it can escape, hide, and strike at will. If you cut off the head of the serpent of evil thoughts as soon as you perceive them entering, they are much easier to defeat. This calls for watchfulness and diligence. It also calls for being fully awake spiritually, and ready to act promptly. It is not obsessive or scrupulous, but it is fully alert in contemplative *hesychia*. Those who have been lulled to sleep by the world or by a false sense of security are often caught off guard. Wake up! And be watchful.

The Spiritual Father or Mother

Key to this process in the Christian East is the role of the spiritual father or mother, and the revelation, or confession, of thoughts. In fact, the East has only recently allowed the Jesus Prayer to be published and taught without the active role of the spiritual father or mother.

This involves a frequent, but usually brief, meeting where the disciple reveals his or her thoughts according to the traditional Eight Thoughts pattern of the Christian East. The spiritual father or mother then gives some advice that is simple and traditional, but also includes the gift of discernment in individual application.

In the Christian West the revelation of thoughts was continued in the monastic tradition through Benedict, and by the 10th century the Celtic monastic practice gave birth to the practice of more frequent sacramental confession for lay people, instead of only a few times during one's life. Today we use both sacramental confession and spiritual direction to achieve this balance. The difference is this: Sacramental confession is only for sins, while monastic confession, or what we often simply call spiritual direction, includes a confident and humble revelation of one's thoughts and temptations to a trusted spiritual director in the West, or elder in the East.

Ideally, the entire spiritual life of the monastic of the Christian East requires the active role of a good spiritual father or mother. Only then can the *logismoi*, or thoughts, be known well enough so that they can be properly treated and healed in Christ. We do well to seek out good spiritual direction for wise guidance in our spiritual life.

But we should end with this caveat from St. Seraphim of Sarov. He says that it is better to have a spiritual director than not to have one. But he adds that it is better to have no spiritual director than a bad one! That would cut a lot of pastoral pain off before it begins! In that case relying on the writings of the Fathers and Mothers can be enough, and God will take care of the rest! This is more common nowadays where good spiritual directors truly rooted in the monastic life and spirituality are increasingly hard to find. However, the active role of a wise spiritual director, or spiritual father or mother, is always preferable.

The Jesus Prayer

It is in Eastern monastic spirituality that we encounter the gift of the Jesus Prayer. I have already taught extensively on the Jesus Prayer in previous books, including a book devoted exclusively to it. So I will only touch on the highlights here.

The Jesus Prayer arose from a desire to follow the Pauline encouragement to "pray without ceasing." (1 Thess. 5:17) The early church used various means to accomplish this. First, they prayed the Lord's Prayer three times a day. Then, people like John Cassian and St. Augustine recommended short "arrow prayers" throughout the day. This would be like, "Oh God, come to my assistance," as found in the Divine Office today. Today we might just say, "Help me God!"

Then around the 5th century, St. Diadochos of Photiki, a bishop in Macedonia, recommended uniting the name of the person of Jesus Christ with every breath we take. Think about it. The one thing we do without ceasing is breathe! As I joke in live ministry, I say that if you're not breathing please have the person next you call 911 immediately!

Eventually, the Jesus Prayer was born. The traditional prayer that has come down to us is: "Lord, Jesus Christ, Son of God, have mercy on me, a sinner."

The prayer was united with the breath, so that we breathe in saying "Lord, Jesus Christ, Son of God," and breathe out saying "have mercy on me, a sinner." We will discover that these words correspond to our breathing. The first part of the prayer is positive, and includes everything in our Catholic and Orthodox Christian faith. The second part of the prayer is negative, letting go of anything standing between us and a full communion with Christ and the fullness of the Church. This not only means theology, Church structure, and sacraments, but real relationships with real people in the Church! The technique is only an aid, but it is time tested, and works well when done well. What is important is our communion with Jesus in the Holy Spirit.

Each of these words has volumes to teach, and our entire faith is contained within it. Let's take a very brief look at the words.

Breathe In

Lord

Anytime we read "Lord" in the Jewish scriptures, it is from the YHWH—the Jewish shortening of "Yahweh." This signifies the vastness of God, who cannot be completely understood, so we cannot even adequately say His Name. He simply *is*.

In Greek the word is κύριος (*kyrios*) and means the "supreme ruler" or God. It's where we get the *Kyrie Eleison*, or "Lord Have Mercy," in our liturgy today.

It gets interesting when we translate either word into English. We use the word from the old feudal system for the head of the manor. The old English is *halfweard* and comes from the words meaning "loaf" and "warden" or "keeper." So the "Lord" is the keeper, or even maker of the loaf.

In my books I unpack this word at length, going through the process of transforming wheat into bread. It includes cutting down the stalk, threshing, winnowing, grinding into flour, kneading into dough, putting into a pan, punching the rising dough, and putting it into the oven. Each step takes us through a series of crosses, resurrections, and anointings of the Holy Spirit that transform us from wheat into a warm, nourishing loaf of bread baked by God though the way, truth, and life of Jesus.

Jesus

Jesus just means "savior" and is also used of Joshua and Jesus Ben Sirach in the Jewish scriptures. But Jesus is a fully divine and fully human Savior who is unique as the full Savior Who is the way, the truth, and the life that all others point to. But we cannot be rescued by this savior if we don't know we're lost!

St. Bonaventure says we are like people who have fallen into a deep and dark pit. Try as we might to climb out by our innate human power, we always end up slipping and falling right back to the bottom again. Bonaventure says that it is only the hand of Jesus that can pull us up and out. All we have to do is cooperate and hang on! Even if we lose our grip, Jesus will never lose His grip on us. I often have the congregation raise their hands, and close their hand around the imagined hand of Jesus to demonstrate this.

Christ

Christ, or Χριστός (*Christo*) in Greek, means anointed. Anointed by what? By the Spirit of God! And we are called "Christians" or

Χριστιανός (*Christianos*), which means "in the company of Christ," or as some have taught, "like Christ." So, we are to be anointed with the same Spirit Who anointed Jesus!

What was Jesus like? The Sermon on the Mount describes His heart very well, as do the fruit of the Spirit in St. Paul's letter to the Galatians. St. Paul says, "In contrast, the fruit of the Spirit is love, joy, peace, patience, kindness, generosity, faithfulness, gentleness, self-control. Against such there is no law. Now those who belong to Christ [Jesus] have crucified their flesh with its passions and desires. If we live in the Spirit, let us also follow the Spirit." (Gal. 5:22-25)

These are the things every human heart ultimately longs for! These are the things that make us fully human, and make life a joy to live! But, as Pope Francis says, "in order to be fully human, you must become more than human." This is the ancient gift of *theosis*, or deification, spoken of by the fathers in reference to what actually happens to us when we are anointed with the Spirit. We are radically changed, and for the better!

Son of God

This points to both the Trinity and the Incarnation. The Son is "begotten of the Father before all ages," according to the Nicene Creed. This means that the Son is eternally begotten of the Father, with neither beginning nor end. St. Bonaventure explains that this is because God is love within His very Self. But love must overflow from one to another to produce a third. Since God is self-sufficient and does not, strictly speaking, need to create anything to fulfill Himself, He must love someone other than Himself within Himself, while remaining One God! So in order to be love, God must beget a Son and "spirate" the Spirit through procession in a union of love within Himself. The Son is begotten. The Spirit proceeds. And this goes on eternally! Now if you think you fully understand that, please let me know, and I'll tell God we have a theological genius and full-fledged mystic on our hands!

I am reminded of the cute story about Bishop Augustine when he was teaching on the Trinity in his cathedral in Hippo. Between services he would walk on the beach by the Mediterranean to clear his head and collect his thoughts. One day while doing so, he saw a little boy digging a hole in the sand, taking a bucket and filling it with seawater, and pouring the water into the hole. He did this repeatedly, and it caught Bishop Augustine's attention. Finally Bishop Augustine asked the boy what he was doing. The boy responded that he was going to take all that water and put it into that little hole! Bishop Augustine responded that there was too much water to put into the little hole. At that, the little boy looked up and said, "Easier for me to take that big ocean and put it in this little hole, then for you to take the big Trinity and put it in your little mind Bishop Augustine!" And the little boy vanished. He was an angel sent by God to remind even the great Bishop Augustine that the Trinity is simply too big to understand.

When we say "Son of God" in the Jesus Prayer, we are reminded of the amazing love mystery of the Trinity.

But we are also reminded of the Incarnation! In his goodness, God freely chose to create the universe and the entire world. He also created the human race. When the human race fell into sin He began the process of redemption by his revelation to the Jewish people. When the fullness of time had come he completed his revelation by coming among us in and through Jesus Christ.

So, when we say "Son of God," we are including the entire life, ministry, miracles, wisdom, death, resurrection, ascension, and gift of the Spirit of Jesus Christ. That's quite a mouthful in three simple words!

But it doesn't stop there. Since the Church is called the "Body of Christ," these words include the fullness of the Church! Plus, it includes the Eucharist, which since the earliest days of the Church has always been affirmed to be the Body and Blood of Christ.

These first words of the Jesus Prayer are enough to bring us to stunned awe caught up to God in mystical rapture. But often they don't. Our obsession with our old self and sin stands in the way. The next steps help us to simply let go of anything standing between us and this full wonder of union with God through Jesus Christ, and the fullness of our communion with one another in the Church.

Breathe Out

Have mercy

Mercy is an amazing biblical word! The biblical word is ἐλεέω (*eleeo*) in Greek, and is where we get the second half of the *Kyrie Eleison*. Biblical mercy is deep compassion united with empathy. It's more than mere sympathy, which, good as it is, remains on the proverbial outside looking in. Empathy is from the inside out! It gets right inside of another. When we ask Jesus to have mercy on us we are asking Him to be inside of us, right at our deepest being.

In fact, St. Augustine said that God knows us better than we know ourselves, because He is closer to us than we are to ourselves! Whoa! St. Paul said no one knows a person but the person's spirit. (1 Corinthians 2:11) The trouble is that through sin we cut ourselves off from a full fellowship with God, others, creation, and even our true selves! When we ask for mercy we are asking God to forgive that severing, and to re-establish deep communion by reawakening us to His presence.

On me

The prayer says "me," not "us." We Catholics are great at community, but we sometimes lack a deeply personal encounter with Jesus Christ.

This simple word, "me," brings out that this relationship must be personal. We can pray for one another, but no one can be saved for us. No one can have that relationship with Jesus for us. We must enter into it ourselves!

Pope Francis gets it right when he begins *The Joy of the Gospel* with, "I invite every Christian at this very moment to a renewed personal encounter with Jesus Christ!" The Jesus Prayer activates an encounter with Jesus that is personal. It brings God, Jesus, and the Church beyond mere words and theories to a personal love relationship that is profound, intimate, and life-changing!

If you do not have that personal relationship, just ask God for it right now! Invite Jesus into your life. He says, "Behold, I stand at the door and knock. If anyone hears my voice and opens the door, [then] I will enter his house and dine with him, and he with me." (Rev. 3:20) Open the door of your heart and soul to Jesus. Pray the Jesus Prayer, and you will soon see a change.

A sinner

As much as I would like to have ended with the last paragraph, I have to include the last phrase! The Eastern monastic fathers added this phrase for the novices, or new members of their monastic communities, who could sometimes get a little overconfident. They could also get so "full of themselves" that they became judgmental towards the older holy monks they had yet to really understand.

They added this last phrase to keep the novices in their place! But it might be good for us, too!

There are several Biblical Greek words used for sin in Scripture. One of the predominant ones is ἁμαρτία (*hamartia*), which means to get off the path or to miss the mark.

Isn't this like you and me? We are created in God's image, so we try to do the right thing. But somehow when left to our own ideas and power we get off the path. We are not God, so we really can't even know what absolute good or evil is, unless we can know every possible outcome into eternity for every action we take. Therefore, our ideas for goodness are often flawed, missing the mark of perfection.

Some people object to mentioning sin in the Jesus Prayer. They would rather focus on the positive than on the negative things in their lives. But Scripture says, "If we say, 'We have not sinned,' we make him a liar, and his word is not in us." (1 Jn.1:10) We must remember that, though we share in unimaginable gifts and glory in our redemption through Jesus Christ, we are sinners who constantly need His grace to get us through the ups and downs of this life.

Saint Bonaventure uses a wonderful analogy to demonstrate this. He says that the human soul is like a mirror created to reflect the beautiful and wonderful image of God. Sin is like dust and dirt that collects on the mirror, first dulling the sharpness of the divine reflection, and then obscuring it all together. The good news is: Jesus does windows! He is able to cleanse all the dust and dirt off the mirror of our souls so that we can reflect a beautiful and wonderful image of God again.

I recommend taking 20 to 30 minutes a day to pray this powerful prayer tool from the Christian monastic East. You'll discover that after a week or so you discern an increase in your spirituality.

Then you'll notice another jump up after 3 to 6 months. You'll see it again after a few years. Finally, after 10 years or so, you'll experience an awakening and enlightenment that follows you through every moment of every day. You will discover that you have begun breathing Jesus with every breath you take. And your life will be radically transformed!

Study Questions

1) Why is understanding the Eastern Christian and monastic tradition important, even for Western Christians and monastics?

2) What is breathing from both lungs, and why is this important in getting a full breath of the Spirit of God?

3) What is hesychasm, and why is stillness important in my prayer life? How do we still our body, breath, thoughts, and emotions?

4) What is watchfulness, and how does it differ from scrupulosity?

5) Explain how the examples of the pond, the spider, or the serpent apply to your prayer life.

6) Do we make use of good spiritual direction from a monastic, pastor, or trained layperson? If we cannot find a spiritual director, do we make use of the writings of the saints to help us?

7) What is the Jesus Prayer? Do you pray it? What are the main lessons you take away from it? Which of the words of the Prayer speak most clearly to you today?

8) Do you have a personal love relationship with Jesus Christ? Have you invited Him into your life? Do you do so regularly?

Mt. Athos

We have already discussed the Eastern monasteries of Egypt, Palestine, and Syria in the early Church in previous chapters. But we have yet to discuss the flowering of Eastern monasticism in later centuries. The quintessential monastic pattern is found on Mount Athos on a peninsula that juts out into the Aegean Sea from northeastern Greece. So, let's end by looking at this wonderful gift from God, not only to the Christian East, but to the entire Church, and the entire world! Technically an autonomous "monastic republic" complete with its own government, it is officially a part of Greece today, though with special consideration for its venerable history.

Mount Athos is made up of 20 main monasteries, plus numerous sketes, hermitages, and even some wandering ascetics who are rarely seen, if at all.

This community was formally founded in 963, when St. Athanasius (not to be confused with the 4th century St. Athanasius the Great) established the monastery of Great Lavra, which is still the largest and most prominent of the 20 monasteries. Mount Athos is largely self-governing, with a capital city and administrative center at Karyes, where a governor serves as the representative of the Greek state.

In addition to the monasteries there are 12 sketes—smaller communities of monks gathered around an elder, but still dependent on the larger cenobitical monasteries. There are also numerous hermitages and hermits in the tradition of the wandering hermits of ancient Egypt. All in all, Mount Athos embodies a very full representation of Eastern monasticism from the major countries of Eastern Orthodoxy.

The threefold pattern is maintained on Mount Athos:

1)   Cenobitic monasteries

2)   Sketes (semi-eremitical communities)

3)   Hermits or recluses

This is the hallmark of Eastern monasticism, and has never been as forgotten there as it often was in the West. For this we Westerners owe them a debt of gratitude. For the West, it took various and frequent reforms to periodically keep such monastic expressions alive. But in truth, in the West we still support them more in theory than in actual practice. The monastic East has kept the full threefold tradition alive and well.

Mount Athos provides a beacon of hope for ancient monasticism today. It manifests the fullness of ancient monastic expressions that remind us that one size doesn't always fit all. They practice unity in diversity without degenerating into a syncretistic universalism or individualism.

But of course they have not been without their problems and need for reforms. In the more recent past the rise of the "idiorhythmic" life brought first great promise, and then great scandal to the Holy Mountain. This was a life based less on the discipline of the ceno-bium, and more on the perceived personal rhythms of the individ-ual hermits and monks in the sketes. This degenerated into monks making a rule of whatever they wanted to do! It is said that you might still find monks who smoke and eat too much meat in the few remaining idiorhythmic sketes. But, praise God, for the most part, these have been brought back into proper monastic discipline by

making them more dependent of the major cenobitical monasteries of the Holy Mountain.

You will also still find a variety of ecumenical disciplines on Athos.
Some monasteries are most welcoming of non-Orthodox monks.
Others are sternly opposed to any interaction at all. In some, Catholic
monastics are welcomed in for their divine services, though they're
still not in full Communion regarding reception of the Eucharist. In
others, Catholics are relegated to sitting on the steps to the church
during any services; they are practically shunned, or tolerated at
best. Hopefully, as Catholics and Orthodox work to restore full
Communion such unfriendliness will eventually disappear into the
fullness of love in the Christ we both imitate and worship.

Study Questions

1)   What are the three ancient monastic patterns, and what
      do they say to you in your monastic or secular life today?

2)   What is the difference between the cenobitical and idio-
      rhythmic patterns, and what is the danger of self-direc-
      tion? What does that say to you?

3)   How do you practice ecumenism in a way that respects
      and ensures the integrity of a hard expression without
      lapsing into judgmentalism or exclusivism?

4)   Why is there a need for periodic reform in monastic life,
      and what does that say to you in your life in Christ and
      the Church today?

CHAPTER 12: WAKE UP THE WORLD

Are you awake, or asleep? Is your spiritual life on fire for Christ and the Church, or are you growing colder as you grow older? Or maybe you are just giving up, and resigning yourself to the ever prevalent mediocrity? But there is hope! And there is genuine joy!

Pope Francis has encouraged those who live in the tradition of consecrated life to "wake up the world!" But he doesn't limit this only to monastics and those living in consecrated life. He wants the entire Church to wake up in Christ! Then we can call all creation to the joy of the Gospel by word and by example.

Quoting Benedict XVI, Pope Francis says that "religious life ought to promote growth in the Church by way of attraction." He goes on:

> The Church must be attractive. Wake up the world! Be witnesses of a different way of doing things, of acting, of living! It is possible to live differently in this world. We are speaking of an eschatological outlook, of the values of the Kingdom incarnated here, on this earth. It is a question of leaving everything to follow the Lord. No, I do not want to say "radical." Evangelical radicalness is not only for religious: it is demanded of all. But religious follow the Lord in a special way, in a prophetic way. It is this witness that I expect of you. Religious should be men and women who are able to wake the world up.

In his Apostolic Letter on the Year of Consecrated Life, Pope Francis encourages three things:

1)   Gratitude For the Past

2)   Passion in the Present

3)   Hope For the Future

Gratitude for the Past

The Holy Father asks us to examine where we have come from. He wants us to look again at the founders' charism in living the Gospel of Jesus Christ.

> The first of these aims is to look to the past with gratitude. All our Institutes are heir to a history rich in charisms. At their origins we see the hand of God who, in his Spirit, calls certain individuals to follow Christ more closely, to translate the Gospel into a particular way of life, to read the signs of the times with the eyes of faith and to respond creatively to the needs of the Church. This initial experience then matured and developed, engaging new members in new geographic and cultural contexts, and giving rise to new ways of exercising the charism, new initiatives and expressions of apostolic charity. Like the seed which becomes a tree, each Institute grew and stretched out its branches.
>
> During this Year [2014-15], it would be appropriate for each charismatic family to reflect on its origins and history, in order to thank God who grants the Church a variety of gifts which embellish her and equip her for every good work (cf. Lumen Gentium, 12)
>
> Recounting our history is essential for preserving our identity, for strengthening our unity as a family and our

common sense of belonging. More than an exercise in archaeology or the cultivation of mere nostalgia, it calls for following in the footsteps of past generations in order to grasp the high ideals, and the vision and values which inspired them, beginning with the founders and foundresses and the first communities. In this way we come to see how the charism has been lived over the years, the creativity it has sparked, the difficulties it encountered and the concrete ways those difficulties were surmounted.

Passion in the Present

Where are we today? Pope Francis encourages two ideas: 1) We should have genuine joy in sharing the good news of Jesus Christ and 2) we should be experts in communion. We should show by example how to re-establish communion, or common union, in a world fractured and breaking down on every level, from the blood family, to the Church, to society itself.

Regarding a favorite topic of this pope, Francis says

> [T]he old saying will always be true: "Where there are religious, there is joy." We are called to know and show that God is able to fill our hearts to the brim with happiness; that we need not seek our happiness elsewhere; that the authentic fraternity found in our communities increases our joy; and that our total self-giving in service to the Church, to families and young people, to the elderly and the poor, brings us life-long personal fulfillment.

> None of us should be dour, discontented and dissatisfied, for "a gloomy disciple is a disciple of gloom". Like

everyone else, we have our troubles, our dark nights of the soul, our disappointments and infirmities, our experience of slowing down as we grow older. But in all these things we should be able to discover "perfect joy."

[…]

From the beginnings of monasticism to the "new communities" of our own time, every form of consecrated life has been born of the Spirit's call to follow Jesus as the Gospel teaches (cf. Perfectae Caritatis, 2). For the various founders and foundresses, the Gospel was the absolute rule, whereas every other rule was meant merely to be an expression of the Gospel and a means of living the Gospel to the full. For them, the ideal was Christ; they sought to be interiorly united to him and thus to be able to say with Saint Paul: "For to me to live is Christ" (Phil 1:21). Their vows were intended as a concrete expression of this passionate love.

The question we have to ask ourselves during this Year is if and how we too are open to being challenged by the Gospel; whether the Gospel is truly the "manual" for our daily living and the decisions we are called to make. The Gospel is demanding: it demands to be lived radically and sincerely. It is not enough to read it (even though the reading and study of Scripture is essential), nor is it enough to meditate on it (which we do joyfully each day). Jesus asks us to practice it, to put his words into effect in our lives.

Hope for the Future

Where are we going? Again Francis presents two ideas. 1) We are not statistics! Bad statistics do not negate hope, nor the belief in marvelous miracles! 2) Our young people hold the promise for tomorrow.

To embrace the future with hope should be the third aim of this Year. We all know the difficulties which the various forms of consecrated life are currently experiencing: decreasing vocations and aging members, particularly in the Western world; economic problems stemming from the global financial crisis; issues of internationalization and globalization; the threats posed by relativism and a sense of isolation and social irrelevance... But it is precisely amid these uncertainties, which we share with so many of our contemporaries, that we are called to practice the virtue of hope, the fruit of our faith in the Lord of history, who continues to tell us: "Be not afraid... for I am with you" (Jer. 1:8).

This hope is not based on statistics or accomplishments, but on the One in whom we have put our trust (cf. 2 Tim 1:2), the One for whom "nothing is impossible" (Lk 1:37). This is the hope which does not disappoint; it is the hope which enables consecrated life to keep writing its great history well into the future. It is to that future that we must always look, conscious that the Holy Spirit spurs us on so that he can still do great things with us.

So do not yield to the temptation to see things in terms of numbers and efficiency, and even less to trust in your own strength.

In Review

In this book we have looked at the "Monk Dynasty" that preceded us and that informs our present experience as we bring the Gospel of Jesus Christ to the future. Let's look quickly at what we've covered:

1)   The beginning with Jesus, John the Baptist, the Jewish Essenes, and the Egyptian Therapeutes.

2)   The first ascetics, widows, and consecrated virgins.

3)   The first informal family monastic experiments as seen in many early Church fathers and mothers.

4)   The Egyptian classical paradigms of hermits and hermit colonies with St. Antony, and cenobitical communities based on Pachomian Koinonia.

5)   The shift from desert monasticism to urban monasticism with St. Augustine and St. Basil.

6)   The balance, moderation, and stability of the institutionalized approach of St. Benedict in the West.

7)   The Celtic integrations of men and women in various states of life—monastics, clergy, and laity—as well as distinct spiritualities.

8)   The 11th century semi-eremitical and cenobitical reforms of St. Romuald's Camaldolese, St. Bruno's Carthusians, and the Cistercians of St. Bernard of Clairvaux.

9)   The itinerant mendicants of the 13th-14th centuries.

10) Finally, the Eastern Orthodox synthesis as found on Mount Athos.

This is a long journey of faith, a very long journey indeed! And it represents a grand and dramatic development as the same essential monastic patterns have been applied in different ways to each era and culture in which the Church found herself.

But this was not the end—far from it! There were still many more developments to come in the unfolding centuries. And the Church and the many communities and spiritualities that flourish within her are still developing today!

So, we started with informal, radical lifestyles of early Christians as individuals or in colonies or families, which developed into formal monasteries with vows. This brought forth the Benedictine vow of stability to one particular monastery for life. Then came the mendicants who vowed the Evangelical Counsels of obedience, chastity, and poverty, to a community that was immediately international, and allowed transfers from one local community and ministry to another.

But this developed much further! Soon we moved from mendicant communities with permanent solemn vows and choral offices, to those with simple vows that technically needed renewal (though made with a permanent intention). These communities allowed brothers to pray outside of choral choir, and sisters to minister outside of the cloister. This stage witnessed an explosion of new communities of sisters and brothers that became the ministry backbone of the Church, especially as she grew with a new missionary energy of the Spirit into the New World.

Next came Societies of the Apostolic Life that committed to promises rather than vows, and allowed for praying the Divine Office individually outside of choir when in ministry. This is where we see the various "society communities" committed to ministry.

In modern times we have witnessed the Spirit raise up Secular Institutes of those who publicly vow the Evangelical Counsels and have a spirituality and ministry, but do not live in formal geographic community.

Lastly, we see the new revival of the ancient categories of diocesan hermits and consecrated virgins who, like those in Secular Institutes, publicly vow the Evangelical Counsels without living in strict geographic community; rather, they live as individuals directly under a diocesan bishop.

But even this is not the end! Today we see the Spirit raising up integrated communities of celibate men, women, singles, and families in one monastic complex, including those who live in their own homes. This takes the reforms and inclusions of previous ancient expressions and applies it to the present for every state of life. This is sometimes called the "New Monasticism," but it's not really new at all. It simply applies ancient principles to our contemporary setting.

This is the form and spirituality of the community God led me to found using existing canonical categories in the Catholic Church as we build something new, yet ancient.

The key word for the spirituality of our community, The Brothers and Sisters of Charity, is "integration." We integrate all religions from a creedal Christian base, all Christian expressions from a Catholic base, and all monastic and religious life expressions from a Franciscan/Benedictine base, which we consider our spiritual mother. But we are still a child that is unique and new. A child loves its mother, and draws life itself from her, but must become its own person as it grows in Christ.

We also integrate the charismatic with the contemplative, the spontaneous with the liturgical, eremitical solitude with cenobitical community, and contemplative community with apostolic outreach. We see the stable Benedictine monastic tradition as our inspiration for our monastic life, and Franciscan mendicants as the inspiration for our ministry.

We are living stones in the spiritual temple of the Church. We must build squarely on the stones that have come before, or we will lean too far to the right or the left, falling to the ground and fracturing our stone. But we must "boldly go where no 'stone' has gone before!" Otherwise we simply imitate previous saints and movements, and vainly try to place our stone where one has already been. But we must build up, not build down! When we have the perfect balance of conserving the apostolic and monastic tradition of the past, and progressing under the guidance of the Spirit today, we can safely build towards the future.

Few see this vision. Most find it much easier to fall into the predictable patterns of the past—left or right, progressive or conservative. These past patterns really have more in common with worldly politics than with authentic gospel spirituality. And they do not bring lasting answers!

Some people think that this vision is "too big," and can easily degenerate into the trap of being "everything, but nothing." But we are fully "Catholic," which means "universal and full." We must be big if we are to fearlessly face the future in a culture that has shifted from a Judeo-Christian heritage to a base in Secular Humanism. We must dare to dream! We must dare to reach yet higher in Christ as we build confidently on the base of the saints, apostles, and prophets who have come before us in Christ, the Church, and our entire monastic and religious heritage. It is, indeed, a Monk Dynasty!

Revival in America

We need revival in America now! We revive America by reviving parishes, and we revive parishes by reviving people, one human heart at a time.

In the past authentic revival gave birth to many new communities and movements. But despite the various waves of the Spirit that have brought potential revival to America, and to the Church in America in particular, this remains one of the only times in history we have not witnessed an abundant flowering of new communities. Does this mean that it was not really the Spirit Who revived us? Or does it mean that we have not properly responded to such Spirit-filled revival? I tend to think the latter. Why?

We Americans cling to our independence—our rugged individualism. But such notions are illusory at best, and only inhibit the full work of the Spirit. We need individuation, not individualism, and interdependence, not independence or codependency. We need individuation that sees every human person as a unique and unrepeatable gift of God. But genuine individuation always sees the individual in the greater context of community. We need interdependence that values each person who freely joins with others out of the strength of a strong self-image, rather than clinging to others out of a weak self-image.

We also cling to professional "job security." So we tend towards expressions of religious life that are more institutional and secure. That's fine for some. God knows that we need to renew old structures as well! But we must always remember that the first monastics were those who dared to step out into the water with Jesus into a miraculous life that had no institutional "job security!" Those who would dare to really imitate the original monastics of Egypt and Palestine are few and far between in today's more professional and job-oriented culture.

Want to Want Revival, or Want Revival?

My experience of Catholics in America is that we often "want to want" revival, but we rarely really want revival itself. "Wanting to want revival" means wanting better results by simply hoping that digging in deeper and repeating past failed patterns will somehow bring better results. Albert Einstein said that this is the definition of insanity! To really want revival requires a willingness, even an eagerness to change past patterns that don't really work.

What past patterns do we cling to, but deep inside we know really don't work? Is it liturgical patterns that might be beautiful, and might even have worked for hundreds of years, but clearly don't work now? Is it lifestyle patterns of consumerism and independence that helped a nation to grow from infancy to adolescence, but have hindered us from growing to societal and cultural adulthood? Is it parish patterns of community, or pastoral styles that used to be effective but no longer really bear good spiritual fruit?

The Monk Dynasty model provides some answers that build on the ancient past, but challenge us to move fearlessly into the future.

Will you join us in this dynasty? Will you be monos—for God, and God alone? Will you gather in a real community that brings answers to a rapidly unraveling Western culture? Will you help us build a better future? Jesus is calling you right now as you read these words. Hear my voice behind the printed words. Come walk on the water with us by bringing the miracle of Jesus Christ to our modern world!

Pockets of Power in Parishes

Many more are called to monastic life than know it, but they have few champions to raise the banner high so all can see. I am convinced that many young men entering diocesan seminaries, or even more active job-oriented religious communities, might well be called to monastic life. But they see no champions for it, so they go, "where the action is." That they respond to a call to priesthood is a blessing. That they might be missing a unique monastic calling is terribly sad. I am raising that banner to you right now! Will you respond to the call?

But after decades of seeing so many come and go through monastic life in our community, and in many others, I am convinced that we will not see revival in monastic life until we see revival in families. Most monastic candidates carry too much American cultural baggage that makes real community life impossible unless it's jettisoned, forgotten, and healed. We must cure the character of candidates before we will see real revival in monastic life.

It is in families that the moral character of children is formed. That's why, despite the occasional saints who came from dysfunctional pasts, coming from a good family was normally foundational for monastic candidates throughout history. Likewise today, we won't see revival in families until we see revival in parishes. That's where good Catholic Christian families are formed. That's why I have spent the better part of the last decade traveling to parishes back and forth across this great nation.

In our community we have seen great promise in our domestic expression for folks, laity and clergy alike, who live our monastic charism in their own homes in ways adapted appropriately for their state of life. We say we want our domestic members and participants to be "pockets of power in parishes!" We want them to be the ones who help form the core of parishes, helping their pastors and lay leaders spread the Gospel of Jesus wherever the need is most acute.

We see this especially with young people! As families partner with vibrant youth movements, many express interest in our community to give them the communal structure and guidance often needed as they grow beyond the initial exuberance of a youth movement into adult life in Christ and the Church.

This also effects our actual organization. Unlike earlier monastic examples that have separate communities for celibate men, celibate women, and seculars in one spiritual family, we have one united community in the Church with separate expressions, united under one Constitution and one government where each is represented. This is unique for our time!

This integrated model seems to be the model of the communities raised up by the Spirit today. We see few such communities in North America, where independence and consumerism grasps so many of us, but they are more fully developed in Europe and around the world. It is not the only contemporary expression, but it holds great promise for the future for those who will dare to respond and help us bring authentic Spirit-led revival to the Church in North America. This revival might be a "remnant revival" at first—that is, a revival limited to a small collection of the confident faithful—but if the few are faithful today, they can be raised in the future into a mighty army for the peace of Jesus Christ and the Catholic Church. Come and join us in the revolution!

A Remnant Revival

As much as I preach that "all things are possible with God," I must confess that I often don't believe that all things are "probable." Possible? Absolutely! Probable? Maybe not. God works miracles, but He also lets us reap what we have sown in order to teach us wisdom. So I follow the old adage: "Hope for the best, and plan for the worst." But I do not lose faith, or hope! All things really are possible with God! Even so, I remain realistic beneath my faith in the miraculous.

And so I continue to preach that "All Things Are Possible With God." After all, that is the title of my weekly TV program that goes out to 600 million homes throughout the week! But beneath that very active ministry, I remain a hermit at heart—and in practice. When not on the road in ministry I live in a hermit's cell in the woods. When I become really content in that solitude then I can safely go forth in ministry. Only then do I not try to possess the ministry that rightfully belongs only to God. Even when I travel I try to create a kind of "mobile hermitage." So my heart is always in the cave, from which I safely venture forth to call everyone to Jesus Christ!

And I must admit that sometimes I wonder if God is not calling me back to the hermitage more exclusively. Our Western world is unraveling. Politics are unraveling. Culture is unraveling. Families are unraveling. Even the Church in America seems to be unraveling! Sometimes I just want to "flee to the mountains." But just about the time I would gladly do so, God calls me back out to ministry. So, I remain a hermit at heart, who also overflows from prayer back into ministry, and leads others through ministry back to prayer.

We are at a "Nineveh moment" in America. We can either repent and prosper, or not repent and perish. The choice is ours to make. Like the prophet Jonah, it would be easy to simply write our culture off entirely and run away. I must confess that I often feel the same way. But God would not allow him to do so, nor will he allow it of me! God had Jonah swallowed up in the belly of the fish and brought back to Nineveh to see their conversion and salvation through penance. So, I continue to speak and preach, calling folks to a renewed personal encounter with Jesus Christ to achieve real revival in America, one parish at a time, one heart at a time.

Having said that, I realize that we might see a "remnant revival" rather than a complete revival of America, or the Church in America, like we have seen in history. This revival might be for the faithful few who hold onto their faith with great love, joy, and peace in the midst of a culture that is unraveling. We might see American culture continue to unravel until little remains. We might also see the Church in America continue to unravel until little remains. But it is precisely at that moment that Jesus will raise us up to walk on water with Him again!

Walk On Water

And this is a good analogy for where we are in history as we come to the conclusion of this study of monastic history and its relevance to contemporary life.

Like Peter, are we willing to step out of the boat of our safety zones in American culture, or in the practices of the Church in America, in order to walk on water with Him again? By logic alone this seems impossible. We say, "That will never happen in my life, my family, or my parish. Have you met our pastor, our Pastoral Council, or our Liturgy Committee?" But remember: All things are possible with God!

Let's think about this: Water, of course, does not look like it should be walked on. Water is for boating, fishing, or swimming—not walking. Yet, that's exactly what Jesus did! And then He invited Peter to join Him on the water. Peter had to suspend his unbelief in order to do so. He had to have faith. Faith is the substance, hypostasis, or "personification," of things hoped for but not yet seen.

So Peter shared in the miracle of Christ, until he took his eyes off of Jesus and onto the storm! When he focused on the storm, Peter began to sink beneath the waves. But Jesus reached to him under the waves to lift him up to walk on water with Him again! Then Jesus corrected Peter for losing faith.

What about us? Will we dare to get out of the boat to walk on water with Jesus? Where are our safety zones? Is it our past patterns of using possessions, our relationships, or even our old self-identity? Do possessions possess us? Do we embrace negative relationships rather than empowering and positive ones? Do we settle for a version of ourselves that is different from what Jesus created us to be? Step out of the boat! Leave the old self and old patterns behind. Walk away on the water with Jesus!

But once we do so, we often falter still. Do we take our eyes off of Jesus and onto the storms of this world, or even the storms within the Church? Do we ever feel like we are being drowned under these waves?

I ask you to extend your hand right now. Allow Jesus to lift you up and pull you up once more from beneath the waves in your life. All you have to do is hold on. Jesus will do the rest. And even if you lose your grip, Jesus will never lose hold of you! He will pull you up to walk on water with Him again! So, step out of your boat. Have faith! Dare to walk on water with Jesus Christ! Then we will see exactly the revival that Jesus wants! Then we will see revival in America again!

This is what it means to be a member of the Monk Dynasty!

FOR FURTHER READING

Chapter 3: The Egyptian Desert

The Desert a City: An Introduction to the Study of Egyptian and Palestian Monasticism Under the Christian Empire- Derwas James Chitty - St Vladimirs Seminary Pr (July 15, 1977)

The Sayings of the Desert Fathers: The Alphabetical Collection- Benedicta Ward - Liturgical Press; Revised edition (1984)

The Lives of the Desert Fathers: Historia Monachorum in Aegypto (Cistercian Studies No. 34) Norman Russell (1980)

The Life of Antony- St. Athanasius of Alexandria, (Cistercian Studies No. 202) Cistercian Publications (2003)

The Paradise of the Fathers Volume I and II–by Wallis Budge (Translator)–St Shenouda Monastery (December 15, 2009)

The Hermit Fathers–by Fr. Samaan El-Souriany (Author), Lisa Agaiby (Translator), Mary Girgis (Translator)- Coptic Orthodox Publication and Translation-St Shenouda Monastery (June 7, 2010)

Monks and Monasteries of the Egyptian Deserts- by Otto F. A. Meinardus (Author)-The American University in Cairo Press; Revised edition (February 1, 1989)

Pachomian Koinonia Volume I-III- by Armand Veilleux OCSO (Translator), Adalbert de Vogue OSB (Foreword)–Cistercian Publications–(1980)

Desert Christians: An Introduction to the Literature of Early Monasticism–William Harmless (Author)–Oxford University Press; 1 edition (May 21, 2004)

Words to Live By- Journeying In Ancient and Modern Egyptian Monasticism (Cistercian Studies No. 207)– by Tim Vivian (Author)– Cistercian Publications (November 1, 2005)

Irénée Hausherr, Spiritual Direction in the Early Christian East, Cistercian Studies, vol. 116, trans. Anthony P. Gythiel (Kalamazoo, MI: Cistercian Publications, 1990; original French edition, 1955).

Chapter 4: Palestine

Letters (Barsanuphius and John) Fathers of the Church Series - Catholic University Press (2006-2007)

Dorotheus of Gaza, Discourses and Sayings - Cistercian Publications (Cistercian Studies No. 33) (1977)

Cyril of Scythopolis, The Lives of the Monks of Palestine- Cistercian Publications, (Cistercian Studies No. 114) (1991)

Chapter 5: Urban Monasticism

Asketikon of St. Basil the Great, Anna Silvas, Oxford University Press, (2005)

The Rule of St. Augustine- Darton, Longman, and Todd Ltd (1996)

Pillars of Community- Kardong Liturgical Press (2010)

A Life Pleasing to God, The Spirituality of the Rules of Saint Basil- (Cistercian Studies No. 189) Cistercian Publications (2000)

Chapter 6: Spread To The West from Egypt

St. Jerome and St. John Cassian: Scripture and Spiritual Life

Jerome. (1933). Select Letters of St. Jerome. (F. A. Wright, Trans., T. E. Page, E. Capps, & W. H. D. Rouse, Eds.). London; New York: William Heinemann; G. P. Putnam's Sons.

Pontius. (1952). Life of St. Cyprian. In R. J. Deferrari (Ed.), M. M. Müller (Trans.), Early Christian Biographies (Vol. 15). Washington, DC: The Catholic University of America Press.

Jerome. (1999). The Fathers of the Church. (T. P. Halton, Trans., T. P. Halton, Ed.) (Vol. 100). Washington, DC: The Catholic University of America Press.

Conferences- John Cassian, Paulist Press (1985)

John Cassian, the Institutes, Newman Press (2000)

Smith, I. G. (1892). Christian Monasticism from the Fourth to the Ninth Centuries of the Christian Era. London: A. D. Innes and Co.

Downey, M. (2000). In The New dictionary of Catholic spirituality (electronic ed.). Collegeville, MN: Liturgical Press.

Celtic Monastic Integrations

Celtic Monasticism: The Modern Traveler to the Early Irish Church- Hughs- Seabird Press 1981

Medieval Monasticism: Forms of Religious Life in Western Europe in the Middle Ages (The Medieval World)- Lawrence- Routledge; 4 edition (April 10, 2015)

Chapter 7: St. Benedict, Balance, and Moderation

The Rule of St. Benedict 1980, In Latin and English with Notes- Fry- Liturgical Press

The Life and Miracles of St. Benedict, St Gregory the Great- Liturgical Press (1949)

Reading St. Benedict- de Vogue- (Cistercian Studies No. 151) Cistercian Publications (1994)

The Principals of Monasticism- Wolter, Herder (1962)

Monastic Practices- Cunningham- (Cistercian Studies No. 75) Cistercian Publications (1986)

Consider Your Call, The Theilogy of Monastic Life Today- Rees- (Cistercian Studies No. 20) Cistercian Publications (1978)

Western Monasticism - King- (Cistercian Studies No. 185) Cistercian Publications (1999)

The Blessings of St. Benedict- Talbot- Liturgical Press (2011)

Chapter 9: The Reformers: Bringing the Ancient Faith into the Now

St Romuald and Camaldolese

Camaldoli- A Journey into It's History and Spirituality, Vigilucci, Source Books, (1995)

The Mystery of Romuald and The Five Brothers- Matus, Source Books (1994)

Camaldolese Spirituality, Essential Sources- Belisle- Ercam Editions- Holy Family Hermitage (2007)

In Praise of Hiddeness, The Spirituality of the Camaldolese Hermits of Monte Corona- Ercam Editions (2006)

Camaldolese Extraordinary- Leclercq and Gustiniani- Ercam Editions- Holy Family Hermitage (2003)

St Bruno and Carthusians

St. Bruno the Carthusian- Ravier, Ignatius Press (1995)

Early Carthusian Writings- Gracewing (2009)

Halfway to Heaven- Lockhart- (Cistercian Studies No. 186)Cistercian Publications (1999)

Carthusian Spirituality the writings of Hugh of Belma and Guigo de Ponte- Martin - Western Spirituality Series- Paulist Press (1997)

The Ladder of Monks a letter on the contemplative life and Twelve Mediations- Guigo II- Image Books (1978)

The Golden Epistle- William of St, Thierry- (Cistercian Fathers No. 12) Cistercian Publications (1971)

They Speak by Silences- A Carthusian- Gracewing 2006

First Initiation Into Carthusian Life- A Carthusian- Gracewing (2010)

The Meditations of Guigo I- (Cistercian Studies No. 155) Cistercian Publications (1995)

The Cistercians

The Cistercians, Ideals and Reality- Lekai- Kent State University Press (1977)

Cistercians in the Middle Ages (Monastic Orders)–by Janet Burton (Author), Julie Kerr (Author)–Boydell Press (August 16, 2011)

The Silent Life- Merton-- Farrar, Straus and Cudaby- New York 1957

Chapter 10: The Open Hands of the Mendicants

Franciscan

The Omnibus of Sources (St. Francis of Assisi writings and early biographies) Franciscan Herald Press (1973)

Francis of Assisi, Volume I-III- New City Press (1999-2000)

The Ideals of St. Francis- Hilarin, Franciscan Herald Press (1982)

The Origins of the Franciscan Order- Esser- Franciscan Herald Press (1970)

Franciscan History- The Three Orders of Francis of Assisi- Iriarte and Aspurz - Francisan Herald (1982)

The History of the Franciscan Order from its orgins to the year 1517 - Moorman- Oxford University Press (1968)

The Complete Works of Francis and Clare- Classics of Western Spritiuality- Paulist Press (1982)

Franciscan Mystic - Brown- Hanover House (1962)

Franciscan Solitude- Cirino- Franciscan Institute Press (1995)

St. Clare of Assisi- De Robeck- Bruce Publishing Company (1951)

The Lessons of Saint Francis: How to Bring Simplicity and Spirituality into Your Daily Life- John Michael Talbot and Stee Rabey- Putnam Books (1997)

Reflections on St. Francis- John Michael Talbot- Liturgical Press (November 1, 2009)

Carmelite

The Carmelite Tradition (Spirituality In History)—by Steven Payne OCD (Author), Phyllis Zagano (Editor)—Liturgical Press (May 15, 2011)

The Mystical Space of Carmel A Commentary on the Carmelite Rule (Fiery Arrow)—K Waaijman (Author)—Peeters (January 1, 1999)

The Carmelite Directory of the Spiritual Life—Austin Chadwell—CreateSpace Independent Publishing Platform (April 19, 2014)

ONLINE: http://www.carmelites.ie/Rule.pdf

Augustinian

Saint Dominic: The Grace of The Word—Fr. Guy Bedouelle (Author)—Ignatius Press (May 2, 2011)

Other Friars: The Carmelite, Augustinian, Sack and Pied Friars in the Middle Ages (Monastic Orders)–Frances Andrews –Boydell Press; NONE edition (October 19, 2006)

Explanation of the Rule of St Augustine (Catholic Classics Book 1)–by Hugh of St Victor (Author), Bro Smith SGS (Editor)–Revelation Insight Publishing co.; First edition (November 1, 2008)

Chapter 11: Eastern Christian Monasticism

The Monks of Mount Athos: A Western Monk's Extraordinary Spiritual Journey on Eastern Holy Ground-M. Basil Pennington-SkyLight Paths Publishing; 1 edition (November 3, 2011)

The Living Witness of the Holy Mountain: Contemporary Voices from Mount Athos- St. Tikhons Seminary Press (April 1995)

The Philokalia, Volumes 1-4- G.E.H. Palmer (Editor), Philip Sherrard (Editor), Kallistos Ware (Editor)-Macmillan (1983)

A Beginner's Introduction to the Philokalia–Anthony M. Coniaris – Light & Life Publishing Co. (2004)

Meditations from Solitude: A Mystical Theology from the Christian East- John Michael Talbot-Troubadour for the Lord (July 1994)

The Jesus Prayer: A Cry for Mercy, a Path of Renewal- John Michael Talbot-IVP Books (August 16, 2013)

The Spirituality Of The Christian East: A Systematic Handbook Volume 1 (Cistercian Studies)- Tomas Spudlik (Authoor) and Anthony P. Gythiel (Translator-)–Cistercian Publications (June 1, 1986)

Irénée Hausherr, Spiritual Direction in the Early Christian East, Cistercian Studies, vol. 116, trans. Anthony P. Gythiel (Kalamazoo, MI: Cistercian Publications, 1990; original French edition, 1955).

Chapter 12: Wake Up the World

The Rule, Constitutions, and Statutes of the Brothers and Sisters of Charity at Little Portion Hermitage - Troubadour For The Lord Publishing

New Monasticism: What It Has to Say to Today's Church-Jonathan Wilson-Hartgrove-Brazos Press (May 1, 2008)

Punk Monk: New Monasticism and the Ancient Art of Breathing-Andy Freeman -Baker Books (June 5, 2007)

The Universal Monk: The Way of the New Monastics-John Michael Talbot- Liturgical Press (March 5, 2011)

The Historical Atlas of Eastern and Western Christian Monasticism-Richard Cemus -Liturgical Press (August 2003)

Hermitage: A Place of Prayer and Spiritual Renewal : Its Heritage and Challenge for the Future—Crossroad Pub Co; 1St Edition edition (February 1989) Reprint Troubadour For The Lord Publishing

OTHER GREAT TITLES FROM JOHN MICHAEL TALBOT

The Ancient Path (Image Books–a Division of Penguin / Random House)

Reflections on Saint Francis (Liturgical Press)

Blessings of Saint Benedict (Liturgical Press)

The Lessons of St. Francis– (Plume)

The Universal Monk: The Way of the New Monastic (Liturgical Press)

The Master Musician (InterVarsity Press)

Signatures (with Dan O'Neill) – (Troubadour For The Lord)

For a complete list visit www.JohnMichaelTalbot.com